HAMLYN ALL COLOUR
GUIDE TO
CATS

HAMLYN ALL COLOUR
GUIDE TO
CATS

Tom Howard

HAMLYN

Special photography by Ray Moller

Designed by Town Group Consultancy Ltd

First published in Great Britain in 1993 by Hamlyn,
an imprint of Reed Consumer Books,
part of Reed International Books Limited,
Michelin House,
81 Fulham Road,
London SW3 6RB
and Auckland, Melbourne, Singapore and Toronto

ISBN 0 600 58014 8

A catalogue record for this book is available
from the British Library.

Produced by Mandarin Offset
Printed in Hong Kong

The photographs on the pages listed below are as follows:

page 1
Brown Tonkinese and kittens.

page 3 left to right
Silver-tipped Tiffany, Brown Tabby and White Maine Coon Cat,
Chocolate Birman.

pages 4–5
Sorral Bengal Cat

page 6 left to right
Blue Norwegian Forest Cat, Blue Burmese

page 7 clockwise from top left
Exotic Shorthair, Tortoiseshell Persian (Tortoiseshell Longhair),
Chocolate Burmese kitten.

$\mathcal{C}$ontents

Introduction

The origin of cats

The cat family has a long evolutionary history but its association with man is relatively recent in comparison with that of some other domestic animals and it remains little changed from the animal of the wild. Compare the huge variation in size and shape which is obvious in the dog – from the Great Dane or the Chow Chow to the Scottish Terrier and the tiny Chihuahua – to the differences between the Siamese and the Persian Cat. While it is sometimes difficult to believe that dogs all belong to the same species there is absolutely no question that cats are all cats. Indeed, the similarities with the other members of the cat family are also strong and it is not without reason that the domestic cat has been called the 'tiger on the hearth'.

The first mammals developed about 200 million years ago, at much the same time as the first dinosaurs, but it was not until after the disappearance of the dinosaurs many million years later that they began to become a major group, taking the place of the dinosaurs. From the early mammals there developed, about 60 million years ago, a group of quite small animals, the miacids. These lived in forests and were in turn the ancestors of all the carnivores, including bears, beavers, badgers, racoons, pandas, weasels, foxes, wolves and the other dogs, and all the cats from the tiger to the domestic tabby.

There were many stages and many false starts before the modern cats appeared, though there was a lynx-sized animal that looked much like a cat around 50 million years ago, which palaentologists call *Dinictis*. Perhaps from this, there developed two lines of cat-like animals or maybe *Dinictis* was one of the early forms after the division. One of these lines was the machairodonts, to which *Dinictis* may have belonged, and which eventually produced the sabre-toothed big cats, some of which would have been known by early man, and in America survived until about 13,000 years ago, although they disappeared much earlier from Europe. The other branch, which did not have the huge canine teeth of the machairodonts, was the family known as Felidae, to which all our modern cats belong.

The felines developed into intelligent animals and fast hunters, and by about three million years ago all the modern cat genera were established, along with other forms which have not survived. The large forms probably arose as the spread of grasslands in the Miocene Era led to the development of large herds of browsing animals, providing prey to exploit, much as the lions, leopards and cheetahs of Africa prey on wildebeest and gazelles today. Other felines developed to live under different

The Korat, with its beautiful blue-grey coat, is a breed native to Thailand, where it has been bred for many years. ▶

conditions and to exploit other prey so that cats of various kinds were found from the northern tundras to the tropics and across all the continents except for Australia and Antarctica and those islands which they could not reach.

Human settlement took cats to Australia, New Zealand and many other places where they had never been known, sometimes with disastrous results for those native species, unused to such clever hunters, which have since been extinguished by the feline predators.

There are some indigenous animals of Australia and New Guinea that have been known by names which include the words Cat or Tiger, but they are marsupials, not mammals, and have no connection with the cat family.

There are now some 35 surviving cat species, some of which have several subspecies. They can be divided into four genera: the *Panthera*, which includes most of the big cats, *Felis*, which includes most of the small cats, *Acinonyx*, which consists only of the Cheetah, and *Neofelis*, which contains only the Clouded Leopard. Taxonomists, the scientists who specialize in the precise classification of animals according to their evolutionary relationships, are not entirely agreed about which cats constitute discrete species. Some think the Lynx should be given a genus of its own, or even group the cats in over a dozen more genera, but the four named are the ones most generally accepted.

The domestic cat is, of course, a member of the genus *Felis*. It was once given a species of its own, *Felis catus*, but is now generally accepted to be a form of *Felis silvestris*, the Wildcat of Europe, Africa and the Middle East. The Wildcat in its northern form, such as those that survive in the wilder parts of Scotland, *Felis silvestris grampia*, often looks very like a modern domestic cat, especially when it shows strong tabby markings. These wildcats and the domestic cat can hybridize, which makes it difficult to be sure that an individual is without domestic blood, but the Wildcat is distinguished by having more bulk, and its tail is blunt-ended compared with the tapering tail of the domestic cat.

However, it is not the Northern Wildcat that is generally thought to be the progenitor of the domestic cat. Influenced, perhaps, by the early evidence of domestication in Egypt, it is considered much more likely that the domestic cat developed from the African Wildcat, *Felis silvestris lybica*. There are several other races of *Felis silvestris* in Asia and it is possible that in some parts of the world they may have contributed to the bloodlines of domestic cats, as may the closely related Jungle Cat, *Felis chaus* of Egypt and southern Asia.

The African Wildcat seems to be quite happy living in the vicinity of villages and homes. Its kittens can be tamed with comparative ease, it is not particularly difficult to domesticate and farmers would have encouraged it to stay around to hunt mice and rats. The European Wildcat, on the other hand, usually keeps well away from people and has only rarely, if ever, been successfully tamed.

The European Wildcat, Felis silvestris silvestris, looks very like a domestic tabby but is almost untameable. Although it can breed with domestic cats, this sub-species is unlikely to have been their ancestor.

Domestication of the cat

When was the cat domesticated? A cat was found by the archaeologists excavating the ancient city of Jericho in a strata dated about 6700 BC, and excavations in the Indus valley produced a cat dating from 2000 BC among the remains of Harappa. It is just possible that the Indian find may be a domesticated animal but the one found in what is now Israel almost certainly was not. However, skeletons of cats found at Abydos, in Egypt, suggest a much closer connection between people and cats. They were discovered in a small pyramid, apparently erected for them, dating from the Twelfth Dynasty (1991–1786 BC). In front of them was a row of offering bowls, which may once have been filled with milk.

These pyramid cats cannot be claimed as pets. They were either objects of worship or treated as symbols of an Egyptian god or goddess. The most important cat deity was Bast or Bastet, who, although originally usually represented in leonine form, increasingly is shown as a cat or cat-headed. These may have been temple cats, kept as her representatives or they may have been used in some ritual – perhaps their actions were carefully watched by priests and their behaviour interpreted as messages from the goddess or as an augury.

The main centre for the worship of Bast was Bubastis at the head of the Nile delta. When this became the capital of Egypt, under the Libyan-born pharaoh Seshonq, Bast became an important goddess throughout Egypt. To Bubastis, and to other centres in Egypt, people brought mummified cats for burial in vast catacombs or for cremation. Archaeologists have found tunnel upon tunnel of cat mummies and pits containing the remains of multiple cat cremations.

Studies of surviving mummies have shown that most of them were African Wildcats but they also include some Jungle Cats. Paintings of cats on the walls of tombs, especially in a group of tombs at Thebes, which date from around 1450 BC, show cats sitting under the chairs of Egyptian women, often at mealtimes, and kittens which are obviously playing with their owners. Again, it is possible that they could have been included for some symbolic purpose – cats were often used as an emblem of voluptuousness and of fertility – but it would seem obvious to conclude that by this date cats were already a familiar feature in many Egyptian homes, and probably had been for many years.

Reports by Greek and Roman writers, especially those of Herodotus in the fifth century BC and Diodorus Siculus in the first century BC, are testimony of the affection and reverence in which Egyptians held their cats. Anyone who deliberately hurt a cat was likely to be severely punished, and when a family cat died the whole household went into mourning, shaving off their eyebrows. The mummified cat would probably then be returned to the goddess as an offering and taken for burial at Bubastis or some local temple.

The African Wildcat, Felis silvestris lybica, is relatively easy to tame when a kitten. It is probably the main ancestor of the domestic cat.

How cats actually became domesticated is a matter of even more conjecture. It has been suggested that the grain stores of the Egyptians would have attracted rodents and they in turn attracted cats. Perhaps wild cats were captured for the temple, where their young reared in proximity to temple priests and priestesses would learn to trust humans. Dogs, being social animals living in packs in the wild, more easily take to following a human as pack leader. Cats are individualists and it is much harder to get them to accept authority. However, African Wildcats may have learned that humans offered them no threat because of the high regard in which they were held for religious reasons. However, if people provided the scavengers around Egyptian towns and villages with food, the cats may have been encouraged into a closer association. Then, since the humans continued to treat them as kittens well after they had reached maturity, the cats may have begun that retention of juvenile characteristics into adulthood which forms the mark of the domestic pet.

Few of the cat mummies discovered in the early days of Egyptology survived and fewer still have been studied. There is some evidence of a cat of a size midway between the African Wildcat and the Jungle Cat – perhaps a hybrid created in the temple populations. Would this have been more easily tameable? Fresh archaeological discoveries in the past decade of large numbers of mummified cats may, when they have been scientifically investigated, shed new light on both the origin of the domestic cat and its domestication.

The spread of the Egyptian cat

The export of Egyptian domestic cats was prohibited but that did not stop cats from being taken abroad, especially when Egyptiana became fashionable after Rome added Egypt to her empire. It was not only Cleopatra who caught the Roman eye: Egyptian religion and such adjuncts as pet cats crossed the Mediterranean too. A lively depiction in mosaic of a spotted cat that has just caught a large bird was discovered in a house in Pompeii. Cats certainly found their way into the Greek world too, appearing on vases and in sculpture in domestic scenes.

At first neither Greeks nor Romans seemed to treat cats as useful animals: their initial appeal was as pets. However, it was probably because of their use in controlling rodents that the Romans took them to all their provinces, though cat bones were among those found in a Roman ritual well beside a temple in Chelmsford in southern England, and in some cases there may have been a religious connection.

The earliest known evidence of domesticated cats in Britain appears to be a single bone dated between AD 10–43, after Julius Caesar's first invasion but before that of Claudius, but that does not tell us much. Paw prints set in the wet clay of tiles before they were fired, and complete cat

Egyptian bronze cat sacred to Bastet, dating from 30 BC.

Ancient Egyptian statue of a she-cat feeding her young.

skeletons uncovered in villas during excavations are proof of cats in later Roman Britain. Whether the first cats came with the Romans or were introduced even earlier by traders, such as those who sailed to Cornwall to trade for tin, we shall probably never know.

Domestic cats were soon known not only around the Mediterranean and throughout the Roman provinces, but in India, in northern Europe, in the Arab world and across Asia into China.

There is considerable variation between the more heavily built cat of Britain and northern Europe and the slim, very short-haired cats of south-eastern Asia. These may reflect mutations in response to different climatic conditions but we know very little about the development of the basic cat types. Some features, such as the restriction of dark colour to the extremities, as in the coat of the Siamese, the taillessness of the Manx, and the different textures of fur in the Rex breeds are mutations which seem to occur at different times in a variety of locations. Although the modern breeds which exhibit these characteristics have been given specific geographical names they have certainly not been restricted to these areas.

The conscious development of different cat types by people with an interest in breeding them did not develop until the late nineteenth century, but humans have played a considerable role in the spread of certain types of cat. Geneticist Neil Trodd has matched the spread of the black coat in cats, which he thought probably first occurred in one of the coastal cities of North Africa, along the trade routes of the Phoenicians, which in the second and first centuries BC stretched from Tyre, in modern Syria, to Carthage and much of the Mediterranean. Perhaps as far as Britain, though modern theories suggest that the Phoenicians' British trade was carried out through Spanish-based intermediaries. The same researcher found a connection between the distribution of the blotched or marbled tabby pattern, which he thought originated in Britain, and the medieval English trade routes across the North Sea and thence down the French rivers that divulge into the Mediterranean. Later British colonial expansion took blotched tabbies to North America and to other colonies and settlements all over the world.

The original colonial developments are often reflected in modern cat populations. The first cats to be taken from Europe to the Americas were almost certainly on the ships of Christopher Columbus. In the areas of Spanish conquest and settlement – Dallas, Mexico and San Francisco – the general population of non-pedigree and feral cats show a predominance of cats like those in Spain and Portugal. To the north, around Boston and New York, cats are much more like those found in Britain and northern France. Across Asia cats followed the silk route, carried by traders to China and then taken across to Japan as Imperial presents.

Later, exotic forms which had developed in the Middle and Far East were taken back to Europe and added longhaired and pointed cats to the western stock.

The Development of the Cat Fancy

The arrival of a new kind of cat, like that of any exotic animal, has always attracted interest as a curiosity almost everywhere, except in the times when cats were persecuted because the Christian church had linked them with witchcraft. However, apart from such influence as deciding which kittens to keep from a litter, there was not much human interference with the look of cats. The decision as to which kittens to keep may have been affected by their appearance, especially if there was a local belief in certain colours or patterns being a sign of the better mouser: one French eighteenth-century author claimed that greyish tabbies with black lips and paw pads were the superior rodent catchers. It was not until the mid-nineteenth century, when more people began to take a pride in their pets and began to exhibit them in friendly competition with other cat owners, that matings began to be planned and controlled.

Angela Sayer-Nixon, English cat breeder, show judge and former President of the Cat Association of Britain, claimed in one of her many books on cats that the first cat show was held in Winchester in 1598 but, if true, this seems to have been an isolated event. Cat shows in the modern sense do not appear to have begun until 1871 when, with the emergence of a group of people in Britain enthusiastic about cats, an artist called Harrison Weir decided to organize a cat show to call attention to the existence of the different kinds of cat and to encourage good breeding practices among cat fanciers.

The first show which Weir organized was held on 13 July at the Crystal Palace, the glass exhibition hall built for the Great Exhibition of 1851 and re-erected in south London. Some 160 cats were entered and the show attracted such attention that interest in pedigree cats became the fashion. Other shows followed in different parts of Britain and the number of entries multiplied dramatically. In 1895 a similar major show in New York's Madison Square Garden made cat shows popular in the USA and was followed by more in a number of other states.

By then Harrison Weir had established the National Cat Club to register pedigree cats and to keep a stud book. The National Cat Club still exists and is responsible for organizing one of the world's largest, if not the largest of all cat shows, held in London every year. In 1898 another British body, the Cat Club, was formed but in 1910 the two came together to form the Governing Council of the Cat Fancy, which until 1983 was responsible for all cat registrations and shows in Britain.

In the USA the oldest cat club is the American Cat Association, founded in 1899, but the largest is the Cat Fanciers Association, indeed it is the world's largest cat registry with branches now in other countries. There are now half a dozen or more cat registration bodies in North America and various other bodies around the world. In Britain, in 1983, a breakaway group from the Governing Council of the Cat Fancy formed

The British Blue, with its plush coat, is a fine example of the British Shorthair breed, almost always showing good conformation.

the Cat Association of Britain, partly because they wanted to see more breeds recognized. The Cat Fanciers Association now also operates in Britain, holding its first British show in 1993. The Cat Association of Britain is affiliated to the Federation International Feline (FIFe, International Cat Federation), established in 1949, to which many other European associations and some outside Europe also belong.

All these cat societies set down rules for the organization and judging of shows and the criteria for the acceptance of a new breed. They all publish descriptions of each breed with which cats should comply – known as the breed standard or standard of points, since they may also specify the number of points to be awarded by the judges for each feature of the cat's appearance and other qualities. Those breeds which individual bodies consider acceptable and the decisions as to what constitutes a breed vary between different cat organizations, and the detailed standards they issue may also vary from one registry to another. In the descriptions in this book an overall summary is given, with the differences between some of the major groups explained. However, if you wish to raise pedigree cats or to compete in shows, you should obtain details of their most recent standards from the cat authority under which you wish to operate. This will ensure that you have have up-to-date information on newly recognized breeds and know of any variations a particular body may require.

The pedigree cat

A pedigree is simply a living creature's ancestry and consequently every person and animal has one. However, there are not many people who know much about their origins beyond their forbears earlier than their great-grandparents without having to do a lot of research. That research depends upon records of births and marriages. The same goes for cats. In practice 'pedigree' is generally used to mean an animal whose pedigree is known and recorded, and for the most part such records are kept only of cats belonging to the breeds recognized by the cat registration bodies or owned by breeders seeking to create new types and colours. Non-pedigree animals may be just as beautiful, loving, playful, intelligent and full of personality as documented cats, the difference will be that their genetic makeup will be unknown.

The advantage of the pedigree cat is that its family history provides information about the type, conformation, colour and pattern of its parentage going back through four generations. This makes it possible to predict with considerable accuracy what its own progeny will be like. By careful choice of mate a particular breed type can be maintained, or modified towards a change that a breeder wishes to effect.

The registration of cats and the keeping of a stud book provides breeders with the information they need to choose the ideal match for

Both the appearance and the spelling of its name have changed since the early form of the Abyssinian breed. This illustration is taken from an 1870's book, 'Cats, Their Points and Classification' by W. Gordon Stables.

their purpose, provided that they also have a sound understanding of cat genetics. Even a carefully planned mating between or with non-pedigree cats, based only on their appearance, can produce quite unexpected results because the cats may be carrying genes for features which they do not themselves display.

Cat breeding

Every cell of every living organism (with the exception of a few viruses) contains a molecule of DNA (deoxyribonucleic acid) and this self-replicating molecule carries all the genetic information which determines every characteristic of the creature to which it belongs. The DNA in each cell nucleus takes the form of a number of linear structures known as chromosomes on which the genes themselves are carried. The number of chromosomes in different organisms may range from one to several hundred but is almost always the same number in creatures of the same species. They are arranged in two strings, the chromosomes along each string being paired with those on the other to control particular characteristics. In cats there are 38 chromosomes, 19 sets of pairs.

In organisms that reproduce sexually, new life consists of a combination of the chromosomes from the parents, taking half from each. Meiosis, the process of cell division which produces the egg and the sperm of male and female creatures, differs from straightforward cell division (mitosis) in that each cell contains only half the number of chromosomes. In this process individual genes may cross from one chain of chromosomes to the other before division so that the egg or sperm carries a random selection from each pair of chromosomes. These are then combined at mating with those of the other parent to produce a full set of 38 chromosomes for the fertilized cell (or zygote) of new life that has been created.

This inheritance is complicated by the fact that genes do not all exert influence of equal strength. Some are more powerful than others for the same feature. These are known as dominant genes, the weaker ones as recessive genes. When a kitten inherits genes of the same kind from each parent to produce an identical pair those instructions are clear and will continue to be passed on. Where the gene from one parent is dominant and the other recessive, the instructions given by the dominant gene are the ones that will be followed but the cat will still carry the information in the recessive gene and it may be the recessive gene which it passes on in the eggs or sperm it produces. Thus it is possible for the next generation to exhibit characteristics not apparent in its parents, though information going back through several generations may indicate to a breeder that those recessive genes may be carried and waiting to have their effect.

The sexes differ in their chromosome pattern. While females carry 19 matching pairs, males have only 18 that match and a further pair which

A wall painting (now in the British Museum) from the tomb of Egyptian sculptor Nebuman, shows him hunting in the marshes of the Nile delta. The cat may have been trained to retrieve the birds Nebuman knocks down with his throwing stick, or perhaps it is there as a symbol of the fecundity of the delta.

consists of one chromosome of medium size, known as the X chromosome, and one much smaller, the Y chromosome – in females it is a pair of Xs. It is a matter of chance in meiosis whether the sperm cell will carry X or Y but when it combines with the egg an XX pair will produce a female and XY become male.

The chromosomes which carry the sexual characteristic carry other instructions too and, because of this, certain characteristics are sex-linked. Most noticeable among cats is red or orange colouring of the fur which is carried on the Y chromosome only. Thus, while a male can be only with or without this gene, a female has the possibility of carrying one red gene and another with a conflicting instruction which may also result in the mixed-colour fur of the tortoiseshell cat. At least that is what is supposed to happen. In fact an exceptional male tortoiseshell does sometimes occur – they have been found to have a Y chromosome and two Xs, but they are almost always sterile.

Although many genes affect only a single characteristic, there are some, known as polygenes, whose function is to modify the characteristics controlled by the other genes. These can be important in determining the length of fur and the strength of coat and eye colours. Some otherwise desirable combinations also appear to carry with them conditions which are to an animal's detriment. White fur and blue eyes, for instance, carries with it a strong possibility that the cat will also suffer from deafness. However, this appears to apply only to pure white cats. Even though the adult may look white a tiny patch of dark fur in the kitten, an indication that it is genetically not pure white, is usually an indication that its hearing will not be impaired.

Cat genetics are not yet fully understood and what is known requires much more explanation than can be given here. Anyone who needs to understand the subject should consult specialist books and learn all they can from the experience of other breeders.

Cat coats and colours

Whilst genetic predictability is the advantage of the pedigree cat, the evolution of all species and the creation of variety within a species has been the result of mutations in their genes. In the wild, natural selection has led to the persistence of mutant forms when the effects of the mutation have proved an advantage to the animal's survival. Human interference with natural selection through domestication may give a mutation that would not be viable in the wild the chance to persist. A colour, for instance, that would make a cat too noticeable to its prey, or a fur type that it could not self-groom. By initiating matings to mix gene contributions breeders have been able deliberately to create combinations that would have been unlikely to have occured in the wild, producing a whole

Illustration from 'The Graphic' newspaper, 1889, depicting 1st prize: 'The Tortoiseshell Tom' at the Annual Cat Show at Crystal Palace, London.

An illustration from the official catalogue of one of the earliest Annual Cat Shows held under the auspices of the Chicago Cat Club.

range of coat colours in cats of a type where there was previously only one. The discovery of an occasional mutant form has also given them the opportunity to introduce cats with entirely new features. This is how breeds such as the Rex-coated cats and the Scottish Fold have been produced. In some cases, such as the Sphynx, which does not have a protective coat, or the Peke-faced Persian, whose excessively flat face could have linked breathing and eye duct problems, the preservation of mutant features has led to considerable controversy.

The Wildcat's coat was originally short. Long fur is perhaps the most significant result of mutation, though not all long fur is of the same type. The Wildcat's basic coat was made up of black hairs striped with yellow, giving the ticked effect it shares with several other animals, such as rabbits and mice. On this coat black areas have produced a variety of tabby patterns: simple ticking, as in the Abyssinian, spots, and the tiger or mackerel stripe, and the blotched or marbled tabby. All black coats were perhaps the first mutation, and black cats may still show spots or stripes in certain lights. Other changes were to lighten the black to a grey, usually called blue in the cat world, to modify black to brown or chocolate and bring in an orange colouring, usually called red. Dilutions from red have produced cream and a combination of blue and brown lilac, also known as lavender. More recently, fawn, cinnamon, caramel, beige, apricot, and indigo have been added to the pedigree palette, while modifications of cream and lilac are known as champagne and platinum.

A dark colour extending along a pale hair creates a number of effects according to the extent of the colouring. When the colour is black a short patch creates a silver effect; a longer one has a stronger appearance with less of the pale coat showing through and is known as shaded, and when it extends further to the root it is known as smoke. This range is repeated with red tipping to form shell and shaded cameo and red smoke. Similar effects with other colours create golden and blue variations.

In certain breeds some combinations of marking colour and base coat colour have been given special names, such as charcoal and bronze in the Mau, but generally marking names refer to the distribution of the pattern on the body. Tabbies have already been mentioned. Bi-colours are white coated cats patched with areas of solid colours. Not less than half, and preferably not more than two-thirds of the coat should be unmarked white and the coloured areas should include patches on the top of the head, ears, cheeks, back, tail and flanks, with a white inverted 'V' on the muzzle preferred. Tortoiseshell is a mixture of red and black for which standards vary, most requiring clear red patches on black but in Longhairs under GCCF rules requiring an intermingling of colour. Blue-cream is a dilute form of the tortoiseshell. Tortoiseshell and white is like a bi-colour with the patches in the tortoiseshell colours, harlequin presents a particular placing of limited bi-colour patches like those which appear in the standard for the Turkish Van.

Siamese cats are the best known of those that display a pointed pattern, with a pale coat and darker colouring on the head, face, ears, tail and the lower parts of the legs and paws. These are caused by related pairs of genes which cause a limited albino effect. This is not white fur but fur from which the colour has been taken, except at the 'points'. Similar genes also produce a silver coat in a similar way by the removal of (usually) yellow pigment from the fur. In the Burmese a stronger effect reduces black to brown. True white is due to a different gene but it is probable that those white cats which have a small coloured patch as kittens really have albino coats. Even bi-colours and tortoiseshell and whites may have their white fur produced by the albino combination.

The standards laid down by cat registration bodies limit the colours and patterns in which particular breeds are accepted and also make rules as to what colour skin should be visible on a cat's nose, around the eyes and on the paw pads to accord with what is thought appropriate to go with the fur colour. Eye colour is also specified. Skin colours are basically black, red (ranging from brick red to pink), chocolate or pinkish brown, blue, lavender or lilac, cinnamon and some midway shades to match the more unusual colours. It is important that show cats should conform to the standards for the registration body in all these respects.

Cat shows

Cat shows are held in many countries, each following the regulations of the body under which it is organized. In Britain they are usually one-day events but in Europe and the USA it is not uncommon for them to last for two days. Under GCCF regulations cats are exhibited in identical plain pens free of anything which could identify the owner because the judges go round the pens to inspect the cats. In the shows run by many other organizations the cats are taken from their pens to another part of the show hall where they are brought to the judges by a steward, or sometimes even by the owner. Sometimes the judging is done in public, though in most European shows the judges work in an area from which the public are excluded.

Cats in GCCF shows are judged in an 'open' breed or variety class and may also be entered in specialist and club classes. The GCCF also holds one special show each season, the Supreme, at which entrants must already have won open breed classes at previous shows. Most cat shows have classes for non-pedigree and part-pedigree domestic pets and even the Supreme has a rosette for the best non-pedigree kitten and neuter. Elsewhere it is more usual to have a series of competitions for Best in Breed, Best Cat, Best Kitten, Best Neuter, Best Pet and Best Exhibit.

The ways for a cat to become a Champion vary. Under the GCCF the cat must win its class at a show and also reach a standard where it is

A colourpoint British Shorthair kitten, with a coat patterned like that of a Siamese, is a recent colour variety in this breed. ▶

awarded a challenge certificate. Three challenge certificates obtained at different shows under different judges make it eligible for the status of champion. If it collects three certificates at this level it then becomes grand champion.

Under American-style rules, a cat which wins the open class for its breed and colour under different judges either four or six times (the number varies according to association) becomes a champion and then goes on to higher stages. Since a cat can win more than once at a single show, championship is achieved more rapidly in the USA.

Entering a show

If you intend to show a cat it must be registered with the appropriate authority and you should have its ownership transferred from the breeder to yourself. Even if initially you have no intention of showing but want to breed a pedigree cat it will be necessary to provide a continuity for the future owners of any kittens. The breeder from whom you get a pedigree kitten may organize its registration for you and will certainly help you to get the application forms. He or she is probably also the best person to tell you about local clubs and shows, though cat magazines and your veterinary surgeon are also useful sources of information. Since posts, except for those of some of the biggest organizations, are often honorary, officers may change and some of the cat registries may have moved, so do not rely on addresses in older reference books.

Attend a show before you think of entering your cat for one. This will give you a clearer idea of what will be involved. Applications should be made as early as possible. Some organizations ask for them three months before the show to give them time to carry out the necessary administrative tasks. You need to prepare the cat for the show so planning ahead is good for you too.

Naturally a cat must be in the best of health and condition. It must be perfectly groomed and this cannot be achieved without prior effort. Again the best advice will come from other exhibitors. You must not pluck out undesirable hairs of the wrong colour, nor use dyes or other artificial means to enhance your cat's appearance and even grooming powder must be well brushed out.

As well as making sure a cat looks its best, it is sensible to acclimatize it to show conditions. The journey, the restrictions of a show pen, being handled by the judges and stared at by strangers can be disconcerting, and a nervous cat will not be at its best. Get it used to being in a pen, to being handled by others, perhaps even play tapes of chattering crowds, and try to ensure that on show day you keep calm yourself – you do not want to transfer your own agitation to the cat. This should be an enjoyable social experience, for you and the cat, not a fraught occasion.

Cat show judges must inspect every aspect of a cat's physique and appearance, before making their assessment.

The breeds of cat

The great variety of cats which have been created from the original domesticated *Felis silvestris* can be divided into three broad types: the shorthair group, derived from the ordinary household cat of Europe; the longhairs, the Persians and Angoras and the Russian longhair from which they may derive; and the foreign and oriental shorthairs, such as the Siamese, but the exploitation of chance mutations has also led to crinkled coats, semi-longhairs, different colours and patterns and a whole range of variations created from the careful combination of these elements. In this book, for the sake of simplicity, the breeds are divided into two groups only: Shorthaired Breeds, including European, foreign and oriental Shorthairs, and Longhaired Breeds.

The various cat associations differ in which breeds they recognize. They have different ways of deciding whether a new breed can be given acceptance and they do not always have exactly the same requirements for breeds they jointly accept. The text that follows attempts to point out major differences but serious cat breeders and exhibitors should consult the standards of the associations with which they wish to register and exhibit. However, minor differences excepted, the descriptions and illustrations will give a clear idea of each breed.

Breeders often make claims for the intelligence and affection of their particular breeds. There is evidence to suggest that blue-coated cats may be of gentler temperament and no one would dispute the lively interest in everything that many oriental cats show, but much of a cat's reaction to human beings depends upon the people who bred it and the attitudes of its owners. Cats certainly have much in common with each other, and that is closely linked to their natural disposition in the wild.

All breeds have their own attractions but in choosing any cat potential owners should be aware of the greater demands which some breeds make. Persian cats need regular and careful grooming, Siamese usually like to be involved in what is going on and do not like being deserted or ignored for long periods. Individual strains may tend to develop a particular character and this should always be discussed with breeders and previous owners.

Kittens often do not look like the adult cat when they are small. Kittens of the pointed breeds are born without the characteristic markings, longhaired cats are usually born with quite short fur and all kittens have blue eyes, whatever the adult colour may be. Some patterns are much less distinct in the young cat, some coats darker or lighter, and allowance must be made for all these factors when you look at kittens.

In addition to the detailed breed descriptions in this book, you will also find that included throughout are helpful, at-a-glance notes on particular breed characteristics, as well as general information on cat behaviour and invaluable tips on all aspects of cat care.

Shorthaired Breeds

British Shorthair

◀ *A Blue Tortoiseshell and White British Shorthair should have evenly balanced patching. The white blaze on the face is desirable.*

A Silver Tabby British Shorthair. The blotched form of tabby is the one most often seen in Britain and probably spread from there into continental Europe. ▶

The British Shorthair is not precisely like the cats of ancient Egypt but more heavily built – cobby is the usual term used to describe its conformation of a low-lying body on short legs. Its appearance is closer to that of the wildcats found in Scotland than to the Mediterranean type. It was developed from the heavily-built non-pedigree working cat of northern Europe, which had become the typical British cat. This was the type of cat most frequently seen in the first British shows before the rise in popularity of Persian cats.

Sturdy cats, British Shorthairs are intelligent and affectionate but usually of a more placid temperament than the cats of oriental type and they generally have a fairly quiet voice.

It is rare for the short dense fur of the British Shorthair to tangle and grooming is easy. Hand grooming, no harder than heavy stroking, will remove much of the old hair but regular daily brushing should be given to keep the fur free of dirt and dust and keep the coat in good condition.

These are compact, well-balanced and powerfully built cats with a full broad chest, short strong legs and rounded paws. An over-long or fluffy coat, a pronounced nose stop or a snub nose, or overprominent whisker pads would all be considered faults.

The blue form, the British Blue, as it is usually known, has a reputation for having the plushest of all shorthair coats and of meeting most closely the requirements of the standard in both fur and conformation, with a good apple-shaped head. Like

BODY

Medium to large, cobby with short, level back, deep broad chest, massive across shoulders and rump, set on short strong legs with round paws. Thick, medium-long tail, thicker at base tapering slightly to a rounded tip.

HEAD

Round and massive with full cheeks and broad skull set on a short thick neck; a rounded forehead leading to a broad, short, straight nose with a not too pronounced break; the ears small, rounded at the tips and well apart, the chin firm and on the same plane as the nose tip.

EYES

Large, round, well open and set wide apart. Gold, orange or copper with most coats, or blue or odd-eyed with white, and green or hazel with silver, green with golden tipped.

COAT

Short, very dense but not woolly or double coated.

COLOURS

Self white, black, chocolate, lilac, red, blue and cream; tabby red, brown, blue, chocolate, lilac, cream, silver, blue silver, chocolate silver, lilac silver, red silver and cream silver, tortie and tortie silver; spotted in any of the self colours, tortie and tortie silver; tortoiseshell, blue-cream, chocolate tortie, lilac tortie, all these torties and white; bi-colour with any of the self colours and white, smoke, tipped in any of the self colours and tortie, golden tipped; colour-pointed in self colours, tortie and tabby colours. The black and blue smoke are the only tipped coats recognized by the CFA, which also calls the tortoiseshell and white the calico, recognizing only this and the dilute calico, not the other tri-colour patchings. Some European countries also recognize an Albino.

other blues, it has a reputation for being particularly gentle. Typical of the way in which changing fashions have been responsible for a modification of a show standard, the blue colour preferred in the early days of the cat fancy was a dark slate blue, but today a medium to light blue of an even shade all over is specified.

The Governing Council of the Cat Fancy (GCCF) treats the European Shorthair as synonymous with the British cat and considers the Chartreux to be the equivalent of the British Blue, although at one time it was shown separately. On the European continent however and in associations which follow Fédération International Feline (FIFe) standards these are considered quite separate breeds and the Chartreux is also given its own breed in the United States.

TABBY MARKINGS

In the tabby pattern, legs and tail are barred and ringed, there are unbroken 'necklace' markings across the chest, a clear 'M' mark on the forehead and facial stripes. In the mackerel (or tiger stripe) type there are vertical lines down the body, but in the classic (or blotched) type there is a mark on the shoulders that extends like the wings of a butterfly, the 'wing' centres showing body colour, and on each flank an oyster-shaped patch surrounded by one or more unbroken rings, with spots on the abdomen.

SHORTHAIRED BREEDS

A male Lilac British Shorthair with the well-rounded face and big round eyes of the British breed. Lilac is produced from a combination of the dilute colours of chocolate and blue. ▶

A Red Tabby British Shorthair. Tabby markings seem particularly dominant in red coats. Red self-colour cats usually show strong traces of them. ▶

American Shorthair

BODY

Solidly built with medium long legs, rounded paws and medium long tail tapering to an abrupt blunt end.

HEAD

Large and full-cheeked, slightly longer than wide with slightly rounded ears, a continuous curve from the forehead over the top of the head and medium long nose.

EYES

Large and wide, the upper lid with an almond-shape curve, the lower fully rounded, set sloping slightly. Brilliant gold except blue or odd-eyed with white; green or hazel with silver tabbies; green or blue-green with tipped silvers.

COAT

Short, thick, even and hard in texture.

COLOURS

Self white, blue, red and cream; chinchilla and shaded silver; shell and shaded cameo; black, blue, cameo and tortoiseshell smoke; brown, red, blue, cream, silver and cameo tabby, brown, blue and silver patched tabby; tortoiseshell, blue-cream, calico, dilute calico; bi-color with black, blue, red and cream and all these in Van patterns.

This tough breed owes much to the working cats which were taken to the USA by early settlers but its pedigree origins go back only to a red tabby tomcat, surprisingly named Belle, sent from Britain at the beginning of the twentieth century, which was the first registered in the USA under the name Shorthair. They were later known as Domestic Shorthairs, but since 1966 American Shorthair has been the official name. This breed is less square in shape than the British Shorthair and has a more oblong head, larger ears and longer legs. Its fur is hard to the touch compared with the soft resilience of the plush British Shorthair. To help strengthen the American differences the registration of non-pedigree cats and kittens was permitted for a time but no outcrosses are now permitted. A specifically American breed, little known elsewhere, it is recognized by overseas branches of the Cat Fanciers Association (CFA) but not by the Governing Council of the Cat Fancy nor the Cat Association of Britain (CA of Britain).

These are medium to large cats with a strong, well-balanced build. Their body length from breastbone to rear should be slighter longer than the height to the shoulder blades from the ground and the tail should be as long as the distance from the shoulder blades to its base. The CFA standard emphasises that they should have the endurance and agility of working cats and strong, long jaws with both level and scissor bites to grip and deal with prey. Mature males should have a definite jowl. Regional and seasonal variation in coat thickness is permitted but it should be dense enough to protect from moisture, cold and superficial skin injuries.

European Shorthair

BODY

A rather stocky cat with a medium-length body set on strong thickish legs with round paws, not quite so cobby as the British Shorthair. The tail, of medium length, can reach back to between the base of the ribcage and the shoulder.

HEAD

Rounded with the muzzle very slightly longer than in the European Shorthair so that it is a little longer than it is wide. The profile has a slight indentation at eye level, ears are rounded and well apart.

EYES

Large, round and set well apart. Blue, orange or odd eyes with white fur; green, gold or orange copper with coats of other colours.

COAT

Short, very thick and firm to the touch.

COLOURS

All solid colours, bi-colour and tabby patterns.

The European Shorthair is a cat that has developed naturally as a European domestic type. Like the British Shorthair, it is robust, strong and muscular but it differs in several respects. It is longer in the leg and should not have a cobby look, and its head is rather longer with larger ears and eyes that are set slightly obliquely.

The FIFe and associations affiliated to it give a quite different set of standards from the British Shorthair and, although the GCCF has tended to consider this an identical cat to the British type, the establishment of the CA of Britain as an alternative registry has brought the FIFe standard into the British show world too.

In some countries, in addition to the normal white coat, an albino colour variety is recognized in which the white coat is due to the recessive albino gene not the dominant white gene: such cats do not have the problem of deafness which is genetically linked to blue-eyed white varieties.

CAT BEHAVIOUR

A mother cat will carry a kitten by grasping the scruff of the neck in her teeth. The kitten will relax and curl its body slightly so that it is less likely to drag on the ground. If someone a cat trusts grips it by the scruff this often seems to make it submissive, helpful when trying to gain its co-operation or restraining it, at the vet's for instance.

Chartreux

BODY

Solid and stocky, medium long, with broad shoulders and a deep chest, set on medium length legs with round feet, which are large in Europe but much more dainty in the USA; tail medium long, possibly tapering but with an oval tip.

HEAD

Rounded and broad but not spherical, a narrow flat space between the ears, which are medium size, set high and slightly flaring, big jowls in the male give a trapezoid shape, wider at the base, a broad straight nose; all on a short and heavy set neck.

EYES

Large and rounded in the USA but in Europe with the outer corner slightly turned upwards; colour deep yellow to copper, with an intense orange preferred.

COAT

Medium short, glossy, thick and dense with a slightly woolly undercoat, mature males exhibiting the heaviest coats.

COLOUR

All shades of blue-grey permissible. The Chartreux has only one colour variety, though its silver-tipped coat comes in a variety of shades of grey.

The Chartreux, known as the Certosino in Italy and the Karthuizer in the Netherlands, gets all these names from the Carthusian order of monks who are said to have kept them, though the modern show breed was not developed until the end of the 1920s and French breeders had pretty well to begin again after the decimation of the breed during World War Two. Blue-grey cats have certainly been known in France for centuries though tales which say that these cats were taken there from Africa by the Carthusians or given to them by crusaders have no factual authority. Though in the 1940s and 1950s the Chartreux were very like the British Blue, and hence were considered by the GCCF to be synonymous with them, they are now distinctly different from both the British and the Russian Blues, and have their own standards in both American registries and the FIFe associations, though they are still not recognized by the GCCF.

It is a more massive cat then the British Blue, especially in the male: both sexes are robust and well-muscled but females are much smaller with a narrower chest and less chubby cheeks. Females may also have a silkier, thinner coat but the longer protective coat of guard hairs should always be over a resilient, slightly woolly undercoat which makes the hair stand out.

The colour of the coat varies from cat to cat and all shades of blue are permissible but a pale grey blue is preferred in Europe and a bright blue in the USA; the uniformity of tone is most important.

Exotic Shorthair

A Blue Exotic Shorthair. This American breed presents a shorter version of the Persian coat but on a cat which retains the Persian conformation. ▶

BODY

Cobby, heavily-boned, of large or medium size, deep, broad chest, massive shoulders and rump, low on short thick legs with large round paws and a shortish tail.

HEAD

Round and massive on a short, thick neck with full cheeks and a short, broad snub nose with a definite break, a full firmly rounded chin.

EYES

Large, round, level and far apart; of brilliant colour to complement coat colour.

COAT

Medium length, dense, plush, soft and full of life; the coat should stand out from the body due to a thick undercoat.

COLOUR

Most feline colours and patterns are acceptable, the CFA allowing cats with pointed markings including lilac and chocolate.

Before the American Shorthair standard of 1966 was established longhaired cats were sometimes used in the development of that breed, with the result that cats of an intermediate type were sometimes produced. After 1966 breeding was deliberately pursued to create this type with the physical conformation of the Persian cat but with short tangle-free fur that is much easier to groom. It is rather closer to the British Shorthair than the American Shorthair in appearance and before the British breed was given recognition as a breed in the USA these cats were sometimes registered as Exotics. This would not now be possible since the nose is broader and shorter than the British cat and the present standard asks for a definite break.

Fur should be noticeably longer than that of the American Shorthair but any suggestion of a Persian-type ruff or of long fur on the tail would be considered faults. Colours accepted vary according to registration body but Exotics can be found in most feline colours and patterns.

Exotic Shorthairs tend to have the placid temperament of their Persian forbears.

CARE TIP

Although small kittens can be lifted by the scruff of the neck, do not pick up an adult cat this way. Always support the body with one hand behind the forelegs, cupping the other beneath the rump at the same time as you lift.

Manx

A *Tortoiseshell and White Manx. Conformation and coat texture are considered to be more important than colour and pattern in this breed.*

A *Black and White Bi-colour Manx. As well as the full or 'rumpy' Manx, some shows allow the 'riser', 'stubby' (with a distinct and movable tail), 'longy' and fully tailed Manx.*

BODY

Solid and compact with a broad chest and short back ending in a round rump, higher than the shoulder; short, sturdy front legs and much longer back legs, paws neat and round. Taillessness should be complete; the CFA allows a rise of bone provided it does not stop the judge's hand or spoil the tailless appearance.

HEAD

Round with prominent cheeks, broad nose and a strong muzzle, on a short thick neck. The CFA specifies jowliness and large, round whisker pads. Wide ears with open base and rounded tip are angled slightly outwards.

EYES

Large and round, the CFA specifying outer corners higher than the inner. Colours conforming to usual shorthair coat colour matches.

COAT

A close thick undercoat with a slightly longer overcoat.

COLOURS

All colours, but not Siamese and Himalayan pointed patterns. The CFA, exclude chocolate and lavender.

The Manx cat, named after the Isle of Man, in the Irish Sea between England and Ireland, is a mutation in which a dominant gene results in taillessness. Foetuses which inherit two of these dominant genes die in the womb but those with only one may have complete or partial taillessness or sometimes a full tail. Tailless cats are therefore usually bred to Manx born with full tails to create the next generation. Unfortunately, the gene for taillessness can sometimes affect other vertebrae or lead to malfunction of the sphincter muscle.

Even tailed Manx have a distinctive conformation, with a short back, short sturdy front legs and longer back legs with the back rising in a continuous arch from the shoulders to the rounded rump. The double coat gives a well-padded feeling and its quality is of much greater importance than colour or markings.

The tailless cat ideally has a decided hollow at the end of the spine. A rise of bone or cartilage there, a lack of double coat or any sign of the abnormalities which affect the cat's health and well-being would be faults. The lack of tail does not seem to affect the Manx sense of balance and its long back legs give it a powerful spring.

CARE TIP

A cat flap enables a cat to go in and out at will. Some have a lock operated by a magnet on the cat's collar – to keep strange cats out.

SHORTHAIRED BREEDS

Japanese Bobtail

𝒦nown for many centuries in Japan and often seen in Japanese paintings and woodblock prints, the Bobtail was noticed by visiting American show judges in 1963 and the first actual cats arrived in the USA in 1968, since when it has rapidly gained popularity. Its distinctive short tail is rather like that of a stumpy Manx but it appears that it is due to a recessive gene which does not carry the risks that go with the Manx. The actual shape is not standardized but individual to each cat, however the effect is that of a rabbit-like scut with the fur fanning out to create a pom-pom appearance that hides the underlying bone structure. It should not measure more than 7.5cm (3in) from the root.

Medium sized, with a well-muscled but slender build, this cat has a distinctive look of its own, especially the head which has high cheekbones, large oval eyes and large upright ears but which is quite different from the typical oriental breeds.

Japanese Bobtails are reputed to like human company, and have engaging personalities and quiet voices. Tri-coloured cats, black, red and white, called *mi-ke* in Japanese, are the most sought after, but a wide range of colours are recognized.

CAT BEHAVIOUR

The cat may use its whiskers to judge whether it can get through a space – they are the same width as its body and are also sensitive to changes in air pressure caused by nearby objects and surfaces.

BODY

A strong muscular cat with a long and elegant torso, set on long slender legs with oval paws, not dainty or fragile looking. The hind legs are noticeably longer than the front legs but are bent when the cat is relaxed so that the back is carried level. The tail can have one or more kinks or angles but should be clearly visible.

HEAD

Long and finely chiselled in appearance with high cheekbones but itself an equilateral triangle with gentle curving lines, set with large upright ears, well apart and at right angles to the head. The nose is long and the broad muzzle rounds into the whisker break.

EYES

Large oval eyes which, seen in profile, show a pronounced slant. They may be any colour which harmonizes with the coat, including blue, yellow, and odd-eyed in white cats.

COAT

Medium length of soft and silky fur and without any noticeable undercoat.

COLOURS

Most cat colours are recognized, with the exception of Siamese type point-restricted patterns and the un-patterned agouti coat of the Abyssinian.

Scottish Fold

The Scottish Fold is born with pricked ears which begin to adopt the characteristic droop when the kitten is about one month old. ▶

BODY

Medium size, rounded and even from shoulder to pelvic girdle with no sign of thickening in legs or tail, and neat, well rounded toes. Long tapering tails are preferred.

HEAD

Well rounded, with prominent cheeks, and blending into a short neck. A firm chin and jaw, the muzzle with well-rounded whisker pads. A short nose with a gentle curve and ears set in a cap-like fashion to expose a rounded cranium, folding forward and downward with their tips rounded.

EYES

Large, well-rounded and separated by a broad nose, wide open and with a sweet expression.

COAT

Soft, dense and plush, so thick it stands away from the body.

COLOURS

Any cat coat and pattern except for chocolate and lavender (lilac) and those with darker Siamese-type points.

The fold-down ears of the Scottish Fold were first noticed in 1961 on Susie, the kitten of a farm cat in Scotland which heads the pedigree of all the breed. Unfortunately, the genes which produce fold-down ears were also found to thicken the limbs and tail and these possible side effects decided the GCCF against allowing recognition in Britain. However, kittens exported to the United States proved sound and healthy and the CFA accepted them for registration in 1976 and the breed gained full Championship status. It has been recognized by the CA of Britain. The breed has been developed by crosses to British Shorthairs and American Shorthairs so their build is reflected in the cat, with a well-padded body and a rounded head. A brief stop is permitted but a definite nose break is considered a fault.

A smaller, tightly folded ear is preferred to a loose fold and a large ear. Kittens have pricked ears at birth and the droop does not begin to show until they are about four weeks old.

Scottish Folds are recognized in a wide range of colours. Eye colours should be appropriate to the dominant colour in the coat. Since 1987 The International Cat Association (TICA) has also recognized a Longhair Scottish Fold (see page 81).

CAT BEHAVIOUR

A cat can use its rough surfaced tongue as a scrubbing brush to reach most of its body but has to lick its paw and use it as a wash cloth to clean its head and ears.

American Curl

◄ *The upright-standing, back curving ears of the American Curl give it a very lively look.*

BODY

Semi-foreign shape with the length 1.5 times the height at the shoulder, the legs should be straight when viewed from the front or rear and the feet medium size and round; the tail should be wide at the base and tapering.

HEAD

A gently contoured modified wedge, its straight nose having a slight rise from the bottom of the eyes to the forehead. The moderately large ears are wide at the base, curving back in a smooth arc with rounded tips. Their interior should be well furnished with hair with tufts desirable.

EYES

Moderately large and walnut-shaped, set on a slight bias, centred between the base of the ear and the tip of the nose and one eye width apart. Colour need bear no relation to coat except that pointed cats must have blue eyes.

COAT

Longhaired cats should have semi-long, silky fur with a minimal undercoat and a full plumed tail. Shorthairs have soft, short fur with minimal undercoat with tail fur the same length as on the body.

COLOURS

All colours and patterns are acceptable.

All American Curls are descended from Shulamith, a female stray from Southern California, which appeared in 1981 with upward-curving ears as a spontaneous mutation. These upstanding ears give a rather quizzical, alert expression to a cat that looks halfway between the shorthair and foreign conformation, is of intermediate size and bone and in its musculature should display moderately developed strength and tone.

The American Curl may have either a longhaired or a shorthaired coat and is accepted in all colours and patterns. The CFA allows outcrosses to Domestic longhair or shorthair for litters born before the end of 2009, allowing plenty of time for the development of this comparatively recent breed.

The ears should not have an extreme curl. Any cat in which the ear curls right back to touch the back of the ear or even the head would be disqualified from competing in any show. The ears should feel rigid and have cartilage for at least one third of their height.

BREED CHARACTERISTIC

The American Curl is one of the few breeds in which short and longhaired cats are accepted within the same breed, as least under the CFA's provisional standard. This may change when the cat reaches Championship status.

American Wirehair

The coarse, resilient coat of the American Wirehair distinguishes it from all other breeds. ▶

BODY

Medium to large with back level, torso well-rounded; legs well-muscled and medium in length and bone, paws oval and compact; tail tapering from the well-rounded rump to a rounded tip, neither pointed nor blunt.

HEAD

Bone structure round with prominent cheekbones, well-developed muzzle and chin and a slight whisker break, the nose a gentle concave curve and medium size ears, wide set and with rounded tips.

EYES

Large, round and set well apart, the aperture having a slight upward tilt.

COAT

Medium length, tight and springy. Individual hairs are crimped, hooked or bent, including those within the ears.

COLOUR

All recognized feline colours except chocolate and lavender and pointed patterns.

This breed is descended from a mutant kitten called Adam, born among a litter of farm kittens in Vernon, New York, in 1966, which had a wiry, coarse and resilient coat unlike any that had previously been studied in domestic cats. It has been described as rather like sheep's wool. Adam was bred first to a normal looking littermate and then to other shorthairs to establish the new breed.

This is a medium to large size cat which may be any of the usual feline colours except chocolate or lavender and those with a dark pointed pattern. The overall appearance of the cat is more important than the crimping of individual hairs but the more dense, coarse and crimped the coat the better, and curly whiskers are also desirable. The density of the coat leads to the development of ringlets rather than waves, especially with longer fur.

SEXING CATS

The sex of kittens and neutered cats can be determined by inspecting the shape and proximity of the anus and the genitalia, viewed from the rear – you may have to lift the tail out of the way. The female apertures are closer together, looking like a dotted 'i', the circular opening in which the male's round penis is hidden is lower; the scrotum, not visible in young kittens, is in between.

German Rex

*F*ur that crinkles and curls is given the name rex fur and all Rex cat breeds have crinkly fur, though it is not all of the same type. Cats with such coats have occurred at various times and places but they were usually treated as freaks and it was only after World War Two that their novelty attracted the interest of breeders. Three types have been developed as recognized breeds.

The German Rex stems from a cat discovered in Berlin in 1951; it has since been discovered that its coat, with the primary guard hairs missing and both secondary guard hairs and down hairs wavy and shorter than normal, is genetically the same as cats which occurred in Cornwall, England, in 1950, and in Oregon, USA, in 1959, but the cat itself differs in other ways. In FIFe associations the German Rex is treated as a separate breed and has a different standard from the Cornish Rex, however, the German Rex is now very rarely seen.

German Rex exported to America contributed to the development of the Cornish Rex, but Siamese were also used in the creation of that breed. The German cat is not so oriental looking and has a round head and round feet.

CARE TIP

Whenever you groom your cat check for any cuts, swellings or other injuries, inspect the ears for dirt and discharges and the teeth for any build-up of tartar which could lead to gingivitis.

BODY

Medium in size and length, a strong chest, rounded in profile; legs medium long and fine with small rounded feet; medium long tail, tapering from a substantial base to a rounded tip.

HEAD

Round with good breadth between the ears, strong chin and well-developed cheeks, the nose with a slight indentation at the base and the eyes set a good distance from it; large ears, wide-based and with slightly rounded tips.

EYES

Medium size, well opened, colour to harmonize with coat.

COAT

Very silky, short and velvety with a tendency to curl and lacking guard hairs.

COLOURS

All colours, including varieties with white, any amount of white permitted.

Cornish Rex

BODY

Hard and muscular, long slender torso, long straight legs with small oval paws and a long slender tail tapering towards the end and extremely flexible.

HEAD

Small and narrow, length about one third larger than the width, narrowing to a strong chin; large full ears, wide at the base and set high, tapering to rounded tips; the roman nose is one third the length of the head and the profile straight from its tip to the forehead.

EYES

Oval, medium to large, a full eye's width apart and sloping upwards. Colour appropriate to coat or, except in the case of the pointed patterned (Si-Rex), chartreuse, green or yellow.

COAT

Short and plushy, without guard hairs, it should curl, wave or ripple, particularly on the back and tail.

COLOUR

All colours are recognized.

This breed is characterised by its curly coat, which was discovered in a cat in the west of England in 1950, the result of a mutant gene that inhibits the production of normal guard hairs and, in some cases, of awn hairs too.

Individuals of German Rex stock contributed to the development of the breed in the USA but the introduction of Siamese and other oriental blood give this cat a different look. Similar curled coats discovered in Oregon and New York State contributed to the development of the American Wirehair.

The Cornish Rex is a smallish to medium-sized cat with a long slim look. The line of its back tends to form a natural arch. Its Marcel-like waves extend from the top of the head right back to the tip of the tail and even the short hair under the chin and on the abdomen is wavy. Whiskers and eyebrows should also be crinkled and of good length. A head of shorthair type or of too long a wedge shape is a fault.

Rex cats do not shed their coats and are easy to groom by hand stroking and an occasional combing.

CAT BEHAVIOUR

A cat rubbing against its owner is leaving a scent mark from glands on the chin, temples and base of the tail.

Devon Rex

◄ *The head shape and ear placing of the Devon Rex are as distinctive as its curly coat.*

The mutation for the Devon Rex appeared in the adjoining county of Devon ten years after the Cornish Rex. The mutation is dissimilar and so when mated together they produced normal-coated kittens.

The shape of the head is also particular to the Devon Rex. The CFA standard defines it as a wedge which, from the front, forms three distinct curves: the outer edge of the ears, the cheekbones, and the whisker pads. With its big eyes and large ears it is appropriately described as having an 'elfin look'.

The cat should be well covered with fur with greatest density on the back, sides, legs, tail, face and ears, the wave being most noticeable where it is longest. Whiskers and eyebrows should also be crinkled, rather coarse and of medium length. Bare patches on a Devon Rex are a serious fault but critics of the breed claim that they often lick themselves bald because their hair is so fragile and embedded in a smaller follicle than in other cats.

BREED CHARACTERISTIC

The Selkirk Rex, not yet an established recognized breed, is a different mutation which appeared in the USA in 1987. The mutant gene is dominant and produces a curly coat which is thick and medium long, thereby giving the usual protective insulation of a normal coat.

BODY

Hard and muscular, slender and medium length carried high on slim legs with small oval paws, the hind legs somewhat longer than the front.

HEAD

Wedge-shaped with a full-cheeked face, short muzzle, strong chin and whisker break, set on a slender neck; the nose with a marked stop and the forehead curving back to a flat skull. Ears large, very wide at the base and set rather low, tapering to rounded tops.

EYES

Large, wide-set oval eyes slope towards the outer edges of the ears. Colour matches coat or, under the GCCF standard, is chartreuse, green or yellow except for Si-Rex.

COAT

Very short and fine, wavy, curly and soft, can have a rippled effect.

COLOUR

All colours and patterns are acceptable.

SHORTHAIRED BREEDS

Sphynx

The hairless Sphynx is a controversial cat. Many bodies refuse to recognize the breed. ▶

BODY

Long, hard and muscular with a barrel-like chest and long slender neck; the tail long and tapered; the legs long and slim with dainty oval paws.

HEAD

Slightly longer than wide, with a whisker break and a stop or change of angle in the profile; large ears.

EYES

Large and round, the outer corners slightly higher than the inner.

COAT

Lacking normal hair; there is a soft downy covering which is perceptible only on the ears, muzzle, tail and the male's testicles. The skin should be taut and wrinkle-free, except on the head.

COLOUR

Any colour is acceptable.

The hairless Sphynx has proved an even more controversial breed than the Rex mutations and those producing folded and curling ears. Its enthusiastic breeders have been met with opposition from those who find it aesthetically displeasing or who consider it wrong to breed an animal they consider disadvantaged by its lack of insulating fur.

A mutation producing hairlessness has appeared on other occasions. A pair of hairless cats presented by local Native Americans to an Albuquerque couple in New Mexico in 1902 were claimed to be the last survivors of an Aztec breed. The modern Sphynx, however, all descend from a cat born in Ontario, Canada, in 1966. It has an unusual conformation, foreign in type, although not of oriental stock, and with a rather pixie-like head. It often has a soft and almost invisible down on the body but its lack of a normal coat means that it cannot tolerate extremes of temperature and must be kept in comfortably warm surroundings. It often sits with its hind legs drawn together to keep its body from contact with the ground. The body feels hot and clammy to the touch. Few registries recognize the breed; the GCCF, CFA and CA of Britain do not.

BREED CHARACTERISTIC

Sphynx cats have no insulation to protect them from either heat or cold. They will often be found curled up against a radiator.

Snowshoe

◄ *A Seal Snowshoe. The breed, developed in the United States, presents a pointed-patterned shorthaired cat wearing white 'gloves' and 'shoes'.*

A Blue Tabbypoint Snowshoe ►
kitten, a variety allowed by those associations which recognize the tabbypoints as an acceptable pattern for the Siamese.

The Snowshoe is another breed created in the United States, and has sometimes also been known as Silver Laces. It combines the body length of the oriental cat with the solid bulk of the American Shorthair, the coat carrying Siamese points but with white paws, as in the Birman cat.

The white markings are superimposed on the Siamese point pattern, ankle high on the front paws and to just below the hock joints on the rear legs. These markings are complemented by a white inverted 'V' on the muzzle which ideally extends up to the bridge of the nose with a thin line of white under the chin down to the chest and along the underbelly.

Developed mainly in the 1970s, it gained full recognition by the Cat Fanciers Federation (CFF) in 1982 and may also be shown with The International Cat Association (TICA), the American Cat Association (ACA), the American Cat Fanciers Association (ACFA), the CA of Britain and in other FIFe shows.

CARE TIP

A cat that goes outdoors should always wear a collar with an identification tag, so that you can be traced if it should be hurt or lost. Collars must have an elasticated section to help the cat get free if they get caught on a nail or twig.

BODY

Long, strong and well-muscled, forming a rectangle with the legs, which are of medium bone with compact oval paws; the tail medium to long, thick-based and tapering slightly to the tip.

HEAD

Triangular, not so long as in a Siamese but longer than the Birman, with high cheek-bones; the ears are large, broad-based and pointed.

EYES

Large, oval, rather like a walnut in shape and slanted toward the base of the ears; sparkling blue.

COAT

Medium short and close-lying, glossy but not fine-textured.

COLOURS

Any of those recognized for Siamese cats by the associations which accept it.

Abyssinian

◄ *A Blue Abyssinian cat, a colour recognized on both sides of the Atlantic. This is the British type; American judges prefer a rounder muzzle and shorter head than this cat presents.*

An Abyssinian displays the clear facial markings of the breed, with lighter fur accentuating the lines on the brow, the dark lines around the eye, and the cheek shading. ►

Abyssinians have gone under such names as Russian, Spanish, Ticked, Hare and Bunny Cat – the ticked coat is like that of a hare and some people were once foolish enough to think that it resulted from a cross between a cat and a rabbit! It was recognized as a show cat in Britain in 1882 and may descend from Zulu, a cat brought to England from Ethiopia in 1868, though there is no firm evidence of this pedigree. An early picture of Zulu does not look much like the modern type which was already established by 1903.

A medium size, muscular cat, which the CFA standard describes as 'regal in appearance', it is not so svelte as the Siamese, being midway between that and the cobby type. North American cats tend to have a rounder muzzle and shorter head.

The ticked fur is distinctive, each hair being marked with dark bands constrasting with lighter bands. The face is marked with dark lines extending from the eyes and up over the brows, cheekbone shading and dots and shading on the whisker pads also being preferred, the eyes being accentuated by a fine dark line surrounded by a light-coloured area. There is often a tendency to white fur close to the lips and lower jaw but this should not extend on to the neck, and white markings elsewhere are a fault. A dark tip to the ears is desirable, and the GCCF standard requires a darker colour extending up the back of the hind legs and as a solid tip at the end of the tail. A darker line along the spine is permitted by the CFA, provided individual hairs are ticked. Barring on the legs and rings on the tail are faults. The belly and inside of the legs are paler, toning with the undercoat.

BODY

Foreign type but more solid-looking than the Siamese, though it should not be cobby, well-developed and muscular; slim legs and small oval paws – the CFA describes the Abyssinian as giving the impression of standing on tip-toe; tail fairly long, thick at the base and tapering, neither a whip nor a kink permissible.

HEAD

A moderate, slightly rounded wedge, brow, cheeks and profile showing a gentle contour and the muzzle not sharply pointed, a shallow indentation forming the muzzle desirable but a pinch a fault; a slight nose break and a firm chin; ears set well apart, pricked, broad and cupped at the base, the GCCF standard expresses a preference for them to be tufted.

◄ *The Ruddy, or Usual Abyssinian, with a base coat of rich brown ticked with black or dark brown, was the original colouring of the breed and the first variety to be recognized. In agouti fur, a feature of all tabby cats as well as the Abyssinian, each individual hair is banded with light and dark segments.*

In some American registries only four varieties are recognized – the original Ruddy (or Usual) colour, with black or brown ticking on rich brown fur; Red (or Sorrel), chocolate brown ticking on warm red; Fawn, light chocolate brown ticking on rose-beige; and Blue, with slate blue ticking on beige, according to the CFA, but steel blue on blue-grey under GCCF rules, shading to oatmeal on the underparts. The GCCF recognizes a much wider spread of colours, including tortoiseshells and a range of silver varieties with different ticking on a silver ground. All colours have an undercoat: orange brown in the ruddy, red in the red, pale beige in the blue and fawn, and appropriately paler in other colours, with white for the silver range.

EYES

Large, bright and almond-shaped, neither round nor fully oriental; amber, hazel or green in colour, deeper shades preferred.

COAT

Short, fine and close lying, but it must be long enough to accommodate double or preferably treble marking with two or three dark bands of colour on each hair.

COLOURS

Usual (or ruddy), sorrel (or red), fawn and blue in the United States; these plus chocolate, lilac, cream and tortie and silver versions of all these in Britain and elsewhere.

CAT BEHAVIOUR

A cat that is warm will often lie with its body and limbs stretched out, even though asleep. Curling up with the paws tucked in and the tail over the nose is the cosiest position for keeping out the cold if there is nobody else to cuddle up to. A cat that lies with its underbelly exposed, like a kitten when its mother washes it, is displaying trust – but beware, a cat that is being cornered or bested in a fight may do this to deceive its opponent and lie ready to deliver a slashing blow with its hind feet.

SHORTHAIRED BREEDS

Siamese

BODY

Medium size, long and svelte;
CFA requires hips never to be
wider than the shoulders, and
a tight abdomen; long slim
legs, hind legs slightly higher
than the front, feet small
and oval; tail long, (and
thin says the CFA) and
tapering to a point.

HEAD

Long and well-proportioned on
an elegant neck, head and
profile being wedge-shaped,
(neither round nor pointed says
the GCCF standard), width
between the ears, narrowing in
perfectly straight lines to a fine
muzzle with a strong chin; ears
are rather large and pricked,
wide at base.

EYES

Almond oriental shape,
slanting toward the nose in
harmony with the lines of
the wedge but with width
between. They should always
be blue, whatever colour the
coat, the more intense the
colour the better.

*I*n 1793 a German traveller reported seeing a cat with darker points, like those of the Siamese, west of the Caspian Sea, but we do not know when this type first appeared in Europe. They were already being shown at the Crystal Palace, London, in 1871 but the first recorded exports of cats from the Thai court, where they had been established for centuries, are not until 1884. Paintings in the Thai archives show slender cats with very limited points – perhaps the result of climate. Siamese coat density is affected by both temperature and age, but an illustration of the cat from the Caspian region shows a heavily-built animal and early show cats were much more bulky than the modern Siamese. There has been a continuous development towards a more lithe animal, so that those known today are extremely slender. The early Siamese also often had a kink in the tail and crossed eyes but these have long since been bred out and would be regarded as a fault. However, a high proportion of indigenous south-east Asian cats still have kinky tails.

BREED CHARACTERISTIC

The points should be clearly defined, although body colour generally shades to a darker tone on the back, and older cats often gradually darken in colour. In torties all must show some break in colour and tabbies must have clearly defined stripes on the mask, ringed tails and barred legs with solid colour on the back of hind legs and at the tip of the tail.

The Siamese should be a medium sized, beautifully balanced cat with long, svelte lines, lithe and muscular. Its pattern displays the albino gene effect of removing colour from the warmer parts of the body, restricting the darker areas to the points, which should show in clear contrast on feet, tail, ears and a face mask. This mask spreads out from the nose and whisker pads to cover the face and links up with tracing to the ears but should not extend over the top of the head.

In the USA, Siamese had become so popular by the end of the 1970s that they were probably the most frequently seen shorthair on the showbench – yet in 1991 hardly any were exhibited. An emphasis on a 'dainty' appearance had produced cats with long, tapering heads and flat foreheads which were of excessive type but increasingly frail, probably because they were confined to an increasingly restricted gene pool. In Britain, where a wider range of colours is accepted, the situation did not occur. However, on both genetic and aesthetic grounds, some people feel that the extreme modern show Siamese has been taken too far and are seeking to reverse the exaggerated look of the most recent cats.

The CFA standard still calls for a more extreme form than that of the British GCCF, asking for the wedge shape of the head to flare out from the nose to the tips of the ears to form a triangle and for the ears to be 'strikingly' large. Several colours based on red or reproducing tabby and tortoiseshell patterns, which are recognized as Siamese in Britain, are assigned in the USA to a different breed known as the Colorpoint Shorthair.

COAT

Short, fine textured and glossy, lying close to the body.

COLOURS

Pointed patterns with a light body colour and dark extremities. Most American bodies recognize only seal, chocolate, blue and lilac points. In Britain red, cream, seal tortie, cream tortie, blue tortie, chocolate tortie, tabby point in all these colours and tortie tabby points are all recognized too – tortie tabbies resemble tabby points rather than tortie points.

Siamese have a reputation for intelligence and can be demanding of attention, making friendly, talkative companions. They often have a loud voice and a particularly harsh call which some people find disturbing.

Siamese cats used to play a part in the funerals of Thai kings. They were placed in the monarch's tomb and when they emerged through an opening left for the purpose it was said that the king's soul had entered the cat as part of its journey to the next life. The cat was then taken to the coronation ceremony so that the late king could observe the installation of his successor.

Although long-established in Thailand, the Siamese pattern did not necessarily develop there and cats with colour restricted to the points have appeared elsewhere.

CAT BEHAVIOUR

A cat approaching with its tail carried high in the air, probably with a curving tip, is a cat that feels confident and friendly.

Colorpoint

BODY

Medium size, long and svelte; a combination of fine bones and firm muscles. Shoulders and hips continue sleek lines of a tubular body; hips never wider than shoulders, abdomen tight. Legs long and slim, hind legs higher than front; paws dainty, small and oval; tail long, thin and tapering to a point.

HEAD

Long tapering wedge, medium size, in proportion to body; total wedge starts at nose and flares out in straight lines to the tips of the ears.

EYES

Almond-shaped, slanting towards the nose in harmony with the lines of the wedge-shaped head and ears; deep vivid blue.

COAT

Short, fine textured, glossy, lying close to body.

COLOUR

Siamese type point markings on pale body colours in red, cream; lynx (tabby) patterned points in seal, chocolate, blue, lilac red and cream; tortie patterns in seal, chocolate, blue-cream and lilac-cream; tortie-lynx points in seal, chocolate, blue-cream and lilac-cream.

This is the breed into which American cat registries put the red and tabby based colour varieties which are recognized as full Siamese in Britain, the tabbies usually being known in the USA as lynx points.

Following Siamese type, this is a medium size, refined and svelte cat with long tapering lines, very lithe but muscular. The head wedge forms an approximately equilateral triangle with no break at the whiskers. When the whiskers are smoothed back the underlying bone structure is apparent.

Point markings are as for the Siamese: legs, tail, ears and face mask, which should not extend over the top of the head or on to the neck but should be linked by lines to the ears. Lynx points should have typical tabby markings on the mask, ears with paler 'thumb' marks, barred legs and a ringed tail with a dark tip. Tortie points ideally have the points uniformly mottled. In both lynx and tortie allowance is made for ghost striping or mottling on the body, especially in older cats.

This breed should not be confused with the Colourpoints, point-marked longhaired cats which are the British equivalent of what some American registration bodies call the Himalayan (see page 80).

Oriental Shorthair

◄ *A classic, or blotched, Brown
Tabby Oriental Shorthair. This
breed, which may have solid or
patterned coats, is a Siamese
without the gene for colour
dilution that produces the
Siamese points.*

BODY

*Long and svelte, in conforma-
tion like the Siamese; legs long
and slim with small oval paws,
hind legs higher than the front
legs; tail long and tapering.*

HEAD

*The head and profile should
be wedge-shaped, neither
round nor pointed. The GCCF
standard specifically states that
it should avoid exaggerated
type; ears are large, wide at
the base and their setting con-
tinues the lines of the wedge.*

EYES

*Oriental almond shape,
slanting towards the nose
with good width between.
Green in most colours except
as described in the text.*

COAT

*Very short and fine in texture,
glossy and close-lying.*

COLOURS

*Self, tabby, spotted, ticked,
tipped, shaded, smoke,
tortoiseshell and dilute forms
ranging through the colours
described in the text.*

These are cats of Siamese type but without the pointed coat pattern. They include self-coloured cats, tipped (in Britain), shaded and smoke coats, tortoiseshell and dilute mixtures, tabby, spotted and ticked coats, tortie (or patched) tabbies and a range of colour varieties – chestnut (in the USA), caramel (in Britain), cinnamon and fawn. These four colours are rarely seen in other breeds although they would be permissible for some breeds which have Any Other Colour classes in which they could be shown. In Britain, under GCCF standards, the self white is placed in its own breed: the Foreign White. At one time the other self colours were also known as Foreign Black, Lilac etc. The GCCF places the Havana with this group, but it is the equivalent of the American Chestnut Oriental Shorthair, the Havana Brown known in the USA is a further development with less Siamese type.

The ideal Oriental Shorthair is a beautifully balanced cat with a long head with width between the ears, narrowing in perfectly straight lines to a fine muzzle, and forming a balanced triangle with no break or pinch at the whiskers, carried on a slender neck and with a long svelte body.

Unlike the pointed-patterned Siamese, all these cats have green eyes, except that the GCCF also has shades of copper to green in the Oriental Cream, Red Cream and Tortie Tabbies and their silver equivalents, and in the Oriental Shaded in its red cream and tortie forms, and excepting the white, which in the USA may have green, blue or odd-eyes.

Foreign White

BODY

Long and slender, well-muscled and elegant, the rump carried higher than the shoulders; legs long and proportionately slender with neat oval paws; tail long, tapering and whiplike.

HEAD

Long, wedge-shaped and well proportioned with width between the ears, narrowing in straight lines to a fine muzzle with a straight profile and strong chin. Ears large and pricked, wide at the base.

EYES

Oriental in shape and slanting towards the nose to match the line of the facial wedge. Clear brilliant blue, the deeper the better.

COAT

Short, fine-textured, glossy and close-lying.

COLOUR

Pure white.

his is a white cat of the same conformation as the Siamese but with no dark points. In the USA it is classed with the other Oriental Shorthairs but is given a separate standard by the GCCF.

This should be a beautifully balanced animal with head, ears and neck carried on a long svelte body, supported on fine legs and feet with a long tail in proportion.

The Foreign White was created by breeding Siamese with shorthaired white cats. Although blue-eyed cats, they do not carry a double dose of the dominant gene for white, with its associated risk of deafness, but have the colour inhibiting gene which creates the Siamese point pattern. Similarly, although their nose leather, eye rims and paw pads are pink they are not albino – although some albino Siamese occur, which are usually known under the name Recessive White.

CARE TIP

To give a cat a pill, grip the head from behind and tilt it slightly back, applying gentle pressure on either side of the mouth with the thumb and opposing fingers, which will help to make it open. Holding the pill in the other hand, use a fingernail to pull the lower jaw down then place the pill towards the back of the tongue. Now, hold the mouth closed until the cat has swallowed. Tubes for dispensing pills inside the mouth are available for those who find this difficult.

Havana Brown

◄ *The Havana Brown has a distinctive head shape and a more sturdy build that distinguishes it from the Oriental Shorthairs.*

The Havana Brown is an American breed developed from the cat now known in Britain as the Havana. In 1952 the crossing of Siamese with black shorthairs, in an effort to produce black-pointed cats, produced a brown kitten, variously called an Oriental Chocolate Cat and a Havana and ancestor of the variety recognized six years later by the GCCF as the Chestnut Brown Foreign Shorthair, a name later changed back to Havana. The British breed aimed to maintain strong Siamese type but Chestnut Browns taken to the USA in the mid 1950s were less 'typey' and they were not bred back to Siamese. These became the Havana Brown whose standards are related more to those for the Russian Blue than those of the Siamese.

The general conformation of the Havana Brown is midway between the short-coupled, thickset breeds and the svelte breeds. A rounded, somewhat narrow muzzle and clear whisker break are distinctive characteristics. In profile the muzzle appears almost square, an illusion heightened by a well-developed chin, the profile of which is square rather than round.

Kittens and young adults often show ghost tabby markings which disappear into a rich, even colour as the cat matures.

POLYDACTYL CATS

It is not uncommon for cats of any kind to have an extra toe. Though a show fault, it may give extra stability and grip.

BODY

Firm and muscular torso of medium length, carried high on straight legs, which are dainty in females and more muscular in males, slightly longer at the back, and with compact oval paws; the tail medium long, neither whiplike nor blunt, tapering at the end.

HEAD

From above, longer than wide, narrowing to a rounded muzzle with a pronounced break on both sides behind the whisker pads; large, forward tilted ears, wide set, cupped at base but not flaring and round tipped, giving an alert appearance.

EYES

Oval, medium-sized and set well apart; can be any vivid and level shade of green but the deeper the colour of the eyes the better.

COAT

Short to medium in length, smooth and lustrous.

COLOUR

Rich and even warm brown, tending to a mahogany red-brown rather than black-brown.

Ocicat

BODY

Solid, rather long but with depth and fullness, athletic-looking but suprisingly heavy, well-muscled medium long legs and oval feet; tail fairly long and only slightly tapering.

HEAD

Modified wedge with a slight curve from muzzle to cheek with a gentle rise from the bridge to the brow; a strong chin; alert, moderately large ears which corner the upper outside dimensions of the head, and with more than an eye width between the eyes.

EYES

Large, almond-shaped, angled slightly towards the ears, all colours except blue.

COAT

Short, smooth and satiny with a lustrous sheen with no wooliness.

COLOURS

Tawny, chocolate, cinnamon, blue, lavender, fawn, silver; all these in silver forms, all patterned with thumbprint-like spots.

This spotted breed began in Michigan in the 1960s with an accidental mating of a Chocolate Point Siamese with a Tabby Point Siamese/Abyssinian hybrid which was then deliberately repeated to provide the foundation stock. Other lines were developed from similar matings in the USA and Europe and some American Shorthair blood was also introduced to add size and silver colouring. Championship status was gained in the USA in 1987 and the breed is now accepted by some European clubs. Though outcrosses to Abyssinians were previously permissible, from the beginning of 1995 only matings to true Ocicats will be allowed.

The resulting cat is of an intermediate type, neither cobby like the American and European Shorthairs nor completely svelte like the Orientals. The coat is tight and close-lying but must be long enough to allow all the hairs except those on the tip of the tail to carry colour bands. The pattern is specific. It features an intricate 'M' on the forehead with markings extending over the head between the ears and breaking up into spots on the lower neck. Dark rims to the eyes are surrounded by lighter colour and there are lines from the eyes and on the cheeks. There are rows of spots down the spine and from the shoulders to the tail and scattered across the shoulders and hindquarters, extending as far as possible down the legs, with broken necklaces on the throat and on the lower legs; the tail has horizontal strokes on top, ideally alternating with spots.

Burmese

◄ *A Brown, or Sable, Burmese. The dilution factor makes this rich brown a lighter shade than the seal of the points of a Siamese.*

A Chocolate Burmese kitten at six months old. In the USA the dilute form of the sable is known as the Champagne and the coat described as being a rich warm honey-beige. ►

There are marked differences between the Burmese breed recognized in Britain by the GCCF and that recognized in the USA, but they both had their origin in a cat called Wong Mau which was taken from Rangoon to the United States in 1930. It was mated to a Siamese and produced kittens that were normal Siamese, some with less distinct points and some that had more evenly dark coats. The latter became the foundation stock for the Burmese, which was recognized as a breed in 1936. Burmese still carry some colour restriction and this is often noticeable in kittens but becomes less so as they grow up.

Unfortunately, the addition of fresh Siamese genes led to an increased Siamese appearance and for a time registration of cats was suspended. It was restored in 1953 when the type had been re-established. It was before this that the first examples were taken to Europe, and, when recognized by the GCCF in Britain in 1952, it was cats with a more Siamese look that set the British standard, although it should still be distinctly different from the Siamese conformation. In France the breed was at first known as the Zibelline.

In fact, cats of Burmese type appear in ancient Thai cat paintings, and such cats occur naturally in southeast Asia; one had been taken to Britain in the 1890s, though then it was thought to be a rare deviation.

Originally recognized only in brown, or sable as it is called in the USA, the colour of the indigenous Burmese, these cats are now bred in a number of colours. In the

BODY

Medium-sized and compact, but well-muscled, with a strong, rounded chest and back, level from shoulder to rump, set on well-proportioned legs with round paws; the GCCF standard also specifies slender legs, hind legs longer than the front, and differs from the American standards in requiring neat oval paws; tail straight and of medium length, tapering only slightly to a rounded tip.

HEAD

Full and rounded on top with considerable breadth between the ears and between the eyes; the American standard requires a broad, well-developed, short muzzle with rounded contours but the GCCF asks for the wide cheekbones to taper to a short blunt wedge; the ears are of medium size, broad at the base and have slightly rounded tips. The neck should be well developed.

USA blue, champagne (a warm honey beige shading to a pale gold tan) and platinum (silvery grey with pale fawn undertones) are also recognized by the CFA. In Britain the GCCF does not recognize champagne and platinum but has nine other colours. Some American registration bodies place colours other than the sable in a separate breed and call them Malayans.

The Burmese is of medium size and with substantial bone and muscular development, surprisingly heavy for its size. It is an affectionate and intelligent cat which enjoys company, both of other cats and of humans. Its short, glossy fur does not demand a great deal of grooming. The Burmese cat generally has a gentler voice than the Siamese.

CARE TIP

The simplest way of giving a cat liquid medicine is to use a syringe. Raise the cat's head, insert the end tube of the syringe into the gap to the rear of the canine teeth, gently squeeze the syringe and expel the liquid. Keep the head raised until the cat has swallowed. Stroking the throat downwards may help this.

EYES

Large and round in the American cat, the GCCF standard requires that the top line should be a straight oriental slant towards the nose; in both they should be yellow to gold in colour with a range through to amber permitted by the GCCF but gold preferred.

COAT

Short, fine, glossy and satin-like in texture.

COLOUR

In all colours the underparts are lighter than the back. Sable (seal brown), plus champagne, blue and platinum in the CFA, and in the GCCF plus blue, chocolate, lilac, red, cream and tortie versions of brown, blue, chocolate and lilac.

SHORTHAIRED BREEDS

◄ *A Cream Burmese, a recognized British variety but not yet an accepted colour in the USA, where the CFA recognizes only sable, champagne, blue and platinum (a silvery grey which is the equivalent of lilac).*

◄ *A Chocolate Tortie Burmese, a colour recognized in Britain but which is not yet recognized by any of the American bodies, even under the name Malayan which used to be used by the CFA for all cats of Burmese type except the sable.*

SHORTHAIRED BREEDS

Tonkinese

◄ *A Brown Tonkinese mother with her kittens, one of which clearly shows the Siamese side of the Tonkinese heritage.*

The darker point markings of the Tonkinese are not distinct, as they are in the Siamese cat. ►

BODY

Medium long with a strong rounded chest and a straight back set on fairly slim legs with neat oval paws.

HEAD

A modified wedge, longer than wide, rounded on top with wide cheekbones and tapering to a blunt muzzle, a slight whisker break, gentle curves follow the lines of the wedge; a slight stop at eye level. Medium size ears, set wide apart, broad based, taller than wide and pricked forward with oval tips.

EYES

Medium sized and more open than oriental, they slant toward the nose. The CFA specifies 'aqua' but the GCCF allows a range from green to light blue but with a pale greenish-blue or bluish-green preferred.

COAT

Short and close-lying; fine, soft, silky hair with a lustrous sheen.

COLOURS

Brown, blue, chocolate, lilac, red, cream; brown, blue, chocolate and lilac torties and tortie tabbies; brown, blue, chocolate, lilac, red and cream tabbies are recognized by the GCCF. CFA allows natural mink, champagne mink, blue mink and platinum mink.

hese are cats like Wong Mau, the female from which the Burmese stem, and some of her kittens; they fall between the types of Burmese and Siamese and have been produced by crossbreeding Burmese and Siamese, although now true bred. Like the Burmese, these are suprisingly heavy cats for their appearance which is of medium foreign type.

These cats have a rich even body colour, shading almost imperceptibly to a slightly lighter hue on the underparts, with darker points and mask which merge gently into the body colour, instead of being sharply contrasted as they are in the Siamese. American Tonkinese colours have their own names: natural mink, which is medium brown with dark brown points; champagne mink, buff-cream with medium brown points; blue mink, which is blue-grey with darker slate blue points; and platinum mink, pale silver grey with darker frost grey points. The GCCF recognizes an even wider range of colour than for the Burmese.

A sociable cat with a coat that is easy to keep in good condition, the Tonkinese is not perhaps as talkative as the Siamese, though usually showing a lively interest in what is going on.

◖ CARE TIP

Groom shorthaired cats horizontally from front to back. Some, especially Siamese, enjoy brushing in all directions and massaging with the fingertips.

Burmilla

◄ *A Black-tipped Burmilla, one of the Asian Shorthair group, has sparkling chinchilla type tipping.*

The Burmilla is a British breed partway between the Burmese and the British Shorthair, which began with an accidental mating between a Lilac Burmese and a Chinchilla. It has the body and head type of the Burmese cat with any tendency towards either the Siamese or the cobbiness of the British Shorthair being a fault. It is a member of what is now called the Asian Group, the name used for all cats of Burmese type, but with non-Burmese coat colour, pattern or length under the GCCF standard.

The coat, inherited from the Chinchilla, is tipped or shaded, both depths of tipping being equally acceptable, with the evenness of shading being more important than its depth. The cat is recognized in both standard and silver varieties through a considerable range of colours.

There should be an 'M' mark on the forehead, lines running from the outer edges of the eyes and pencilling on the cheeks, but shading on the body should be as free of tabby markings as possible, with denser colour along the spine and down the tail, dispersing gradually to become as light as possible on the underparts. The tail should be marked with incomplete rings and have a dark tip, the paws slightly barred, light spotting is permitted on the belly. The eyes should be outlined like those of the Chinchilla, the visible skin matching the coat colour.

BODY

Medium length and thickness with firm muscle, a straight back and a generous but not disproportionately broad chest; legs medium length, the hind legs slightly longer than the front, paws tending to an oval shape; tail medium to long, medium thick, tapering slightly to a rounded tip.

HEAD

A short wedge with a distinct nose break apparent in profile, width between the ears which are medium to large, round tipped and continue the angle of the upper part of the face to produce a butterfly-wing outline from the front.

EYES

Full, well apart and slightly oriental in set but neither almond nor round; colour yellow through to chartreuse, except in silver-coated cats for which green is preferred.

COAT

Short, fine and close-lying, slight ear tufts acceptable.

COLOUR

Black, blue, chocolate, lilac, red, caramel, apricot, cream; black, blue, chocolate, lilac or caramel tortie; any of these colours with a Burmese colour restriction and any of these in silver form.

Russian Blue

A British-bred Russian Blue. American bred cats have round eyes and the nose leather would be slate grey. ▶

BODY

Long and graceful in outline and carriage with long legs and small oval feet; the tail long and tapering, neither blunt ended nor whip-like.

HEAD

A smooth short wedge with a flat appearance between the ears; forehead and nose are straight in profile, meeting at an angle with the upper edge of the eye with no nose break or stop; whisker pads are prominent, ears large, pointed, wide at their base and set vertically and well apart.

EYES

Vivid green and set wide apart, almond-shaped under GCCF standards, but the CFA ask for round eyes.

COAT

Double, soft, thick and very fine; it stands up very soft and silky, different in texture from any other breed.

COLOUR

An even bright blue throughout; a medium shade is preferred by the GCCF, lighter shades by the CFA. Silver tipping to the guard hairs gives the special sheen.

The Russian Blue seems to be a breed that has developed naturally, not one created by breeders in search of a particular look. It may even be the Archangel Cat, a type which English sailors are said to have taken home from Russia in the sixteenth century, though in the seventeenth century blue cats were called Maltese, a name by which they were also known in the USA. In Britain, in the early days of the Cat Fancy, cats called Russian, Spanish, Maltese and Archangel were shown alongside the British Blue but in 1912 the Russian (or Foreign as it was then called) gained a separate class.

After World War Two the stock in Britain was so low that Siamese blood was introduced and for a time the British standard required a Siamese type but on both sides of the Atlantic a Siamese-looking cat would now be undesirable. American and British GCCF standards still require different eye shapes, with blue nose leather and paw pads in Britain, slate grey and lavender pink in the USA, and a lighter shade of coat preferred in the USA too.

The double coat with its silver sheen is particular to the breed. In Britain Russian White and Russian Black varieties have been developed to identical standards, except for coat colour.

Asian Smoke/Tabby

BODY

Medium length and thickness with firm muscle, a straight back and a generous but not disproportionately broad chest; legs medium length, the hind legs slightly longer than the front, paws tending to an oval shape; tail medium to long, medium thick, tapering slightly to a rounded tip.

HEAD

A short wedge with a distinct nose break apparent in profile, width between the ears which are medium to large, round-tipped and continue the angle of the upper part of the face to produce a butterfly-wing outline from the front.

EYES

Full, well apart and slightly oriental in set but neither almond nor round; colour yellow through to chartreuse, except in silver-coated cats for which green is preferred.

COAT

Short, fine and close-lying, slight ear tufts acceptable.

COLOUR

Black, blue, chocolate, lilac, red, caramel, apricot, cream; black, blue, chocolate, lilac or caramel tortie; any of these colours with a Burmese colour restriction and any of these in silver form.

Like the Burmilla, the Asian Smoke and the Asian Tabby are part of the Asian Shorthair Group and are covered by the same general standard.

The Smoke was first developed in Britain under the name Burmoire. It does not have the normal tabby's colour-banded 'agouti' fur although it carries some tabby markings. The coat may be any of the colours in the same range as the Burmilla, including those with Burmese colour restriction, with a silvery-white or near white undercoat. In adults this should be approximately one-third to one-half of the total length of each hair but presenting a full-coloured surface, typical of smokes. However, there should also be silvery frown marks on the forehead and silvery rings around the eyes. Ghost tabby markings on the body give the effect of watered silk.

The Asian Tabby comes in Ticked, Spotted, Mackerel and Classic (blotched) forms in a similar colour range. In the Ticked the agouti pattern should produce an even ticking of two or three bands of darker colour extending well down each hair, the face marked with a forehead 'M' and pencilling, the tail and legs tabby marked, and a dark line down the spine. Asian Spotted Tabbies should have clear spots without agouti hairs, no dark line on the spine but face, legs and tail carrying tabby marks. Classic and Mackerel Tabbies follow the usual requirement for these patterns.

Bombay

The Bombay, classed with the Asian Shorthairs in Britain but recognized as a breed in its own right in the USA. ▶

BODY

Medium size, muscular in development, neither compact nor rangy, with a tail which is straight, medium long and not 'whippy' and legs in proportion set on round paws.

HEAD

Pleasingly rounded with no sharp angles, face full with considerable breadth between the eyes, tapering slightly to a short, well-developed muzzle, with a nose break which is visible in profile.

EYES

Rounded and set far apart.

COAT

Fine, short, satin-like texture with a shimmering patent leather sheen.

COLOUR

Black to the roots.

The Bombay was developed in the United States, where it was granted Championship status by the CFA in 1976. It was the result of crossing Black American Shorthairs with Burmese of the American type and has the Burmese characteristic of looking lighter than it is. Its solid body and what the CFA standard calls 'a sweet facial expression' combine with jet black gleaming fur and bright gold or vivid copper eyes to give this friendly, personable breed a look of its own.

Fur must be black to the roots. Kittens may take some time to develop the full dark colour but they become more sleek with age to reach what the British and American standards both liken to a 'shimmering patent leather'. The eyes too have a special brilliance when set off by the sleek black coat.

In Britain, the Bombay standard is as for the other Asian Group shorthaired cats, except for its restriction to a single colour.

Nose leather, eye rims and paw pads should all be solid black, with very dark brown paw pads also acceptable under the GCCF.

In Britain the GCCF standard is as for the Burmilla and other Asian types. In the USA it is as set out in the breed description to the left.

Egyptian Mau

◀ *The Egyptian Mau, developed from genuine Egyptian spotted cats, recalls the pets depicted in ancient Egyptian art.*

BODY

Medium long and graceful, but with well-developed muscle; legs and feet in proportion with hind legs longer, giving the appearance of being on tiptoe when standing upright; small, dainty feet, very slightly oval; tail medium long, thick at base with slight taper.

HEAD

Medium long, slightly rounded wedge with no flat planes, not full cheeked, nose of even width throughout its length when seen from front, and profile showing a gentle contour with a slight rise from nose bridge to forehead; ears medium to large, alert and moderately pointed, broad based with ample width between them; the inner ear is a delicate almost transparent pink.

EYES

Large, almond-shaped with a slight slant towards the ears, and a light 'gooseberry' green in colour.

COAT

Medium length with a lustrous sheen, ears may be tufted; dense and resilient in silver and bronze coats, silky and fine in smokes.

COLOURS

Silver, bronze and smoke.

The Egyptian Mau was an attempt to establish from a naturally occurring indigenous spotted cat a breed resembling the cats depicted in ancient Egyptian art. The Mau developed from a silver spotted female from Egypt, which was taken to Rome in the 1950s and mated to another Egyptian cat, a smoke spotted tom, which had arrived earlier. Their kittens, after being entered in a show in Rome, were taken to the USA where the breed eventually received recognition in 1968.

The Mau has an oriental look combined with a more cobby build, more like the Abyssinian than the Siamese. The fur is randomly spotted with distinct markings of varying size and shape on a paler ground. The cheeks are barred with a line from the eye along the contour of the cheek and another curving upwards from the centre of the cheek. The forehead carries a clear 'M' and frown marks forming lines between the ears which extend down the back of the neck breaking into elongated spots along the spine. There are one or more broken 'necklace' markings on the upper chest, shoulder markings and those on the haunches and upper hind legs are transitional between stripes and spots, legs are barred and the tail ringed with a dark tip. Silver cats have charcoal spotting on a pale silver ground; bronze dark brown-black on a coppery brown, fading to creamy ivory on the underside; smoke jet black on a pale silver ground with a white to pale silver undercoat.

In Britain the name Mau was originally used for a range of spotted cats bred experimentally in the 1960s. These were not based on Egyptian stock and have now been established under the name Oriental Tabbies.

Korat

The Korat has a unique coat that does not show its full splendour until the cat is fully grown. ▶

BODY

Medium size, semi-cobby, neither compact nor svelte, broad chested and muscular, the back carried in a curve; height from base of tail to ground equal to distance from nape to base of tail, front legs shorter than back, paws oval; tail medium long, heavier at base, tapering to a rounded tip.

HEAD

Heart-shaped from front, broad between and across the eyes, curves gently to a well-developed but neither over-square nor sharp-pointed chin; short nose with slight stop; large ears, high set, flaring at the base and round tipped.

EYES

Large and prominent, round when fully open but with an oriental slant when partly closed, colour a brilliant green.

COAT

Short (short to medium in the GCCF standard), single, glossy, fine and close-lying. Over the spine it tends to part as the cat moves.

COLOUR

Any shade of blue in GCCF standard, silver blue in CFA, always tipped with silver. Shorter coats intensify the silver sheen.

This is a breed indigenous to Thailand, where it is regarded as a bringer of good luck. One was shown in London in 1896 but it was not until 1959, when a pair were taken to the USA, that it attracted the attention of the Cat Fancy, receiving American recognition in 1966 and British in 1975.

Medium sized and semi-cobby, the Korat has a distinctive heart-shaped face, the eyebrow ridges forming the upper curves of the heart and the sides gently curving down to a strong and well-developed chin. The forehead is large and flat.

There is only one colour variety, with a blue to silver blue coat tipped with silver. The roots of the hair are usually lighter, the colour intensifying to be deepest just before the silver tip. An ancient Thai poet described it as having 'roots like clouds and tips like silver' and said that the cat's eyes 'shine like dewdrops in a lotus leaf'. The luminous green eyes are wide open and large in proportion to the face. Kittens have yellow to greenish-amber eyes and do not gain adult colour until two or more years old. The kitten's coat does not exhibit the typical strong tipping which develops gradually as the cat matures.

CARE TIP

A bored cat can become a destructive cat, so always make time to give your cat regular attention and to play games that it enjoys.

Bengal

This breed is the result of a cross between the spotted feral domestic cats and one of the wild species, *Felis bengalensis*, the Leopard Cat of southeast Asia, which occurs from Siberia and Kashmir to Bali. The breeder's aim was to keep its dark spotted patterning of body and legs, and the black bands running over the forehead. The spots, despite the 'leopard' appellation, are solid, and not like the open rosettes of the larger cat.

Males from initial matings proved sterile, but females were then mated with a red feral cat with brown spotting, found living in Delhi Zoo, and with a brown spotted tabby from a Los Angeles cat shelter.

Previous hybrids between wild and domestic cats have usually resulted in rather aggressive kittens, difficult to keep as pets, but Bengal breeders claim that they have managed to retain the gentleness of the domestic cat while giving it the exotic look of a leopard-like coat.

CAT BEHAVIOUR

A cat often sits with its mouth partly open, giving a rather scornful expression, in what zoologists call the flehmen reaction. It is drawing air into its mouth and up through a special scent organ, the better to identify and enjoy some interesting smell.

BODY

Long, thick and heavily-muscled with strong legs and unusually large feet; tail carried low.

HEAD

Rather large in proportion to the body; nostrils sometimes slightly bulbous; ears small and rounded.

EYES

Slightly oblique and well apart; yellow.

COAT

Texture more pelt-like than the usual domestic cat, resembling that of the Leopard Cat.

COLOURS

Leopard (black spots on bright orange), sorrel (brown on lighter orange), mink (black on rich mahogany).

SHORTHAIRED BREEDS

Singapura

BODY

Small to medium size, stocky and muscular, set on heavy legs tapering to small oval paws; tail medium long with a blunt tip.

HEAD

Rounded with a medium length muzzle, blunt nose, strong chin and definite whisker break and large, slightly pointed ears. In profile the rounded skull shows a slight stop well below the level of the eyes.

EYES

Large and almond-shaped, hazel green or yellow in colour.

COAT

Short and fine, with at least two bands of ticking.

COLOUR

Sepia agouti only.

The Singapura was developed by an American breeder from cats she discovered in Singapore and took back to the United States, where a careful breeding programme developed a breed that found acceptance.

The muscular-bodied Singapura is of medium size with noticeably large eyes, not less than an eye-width apart, and deeply cupped, medium set ears with their outer lines extending upward at an angle slightly wide of parallel. Body and legs should form a square with the ground; the mid-section should be firm and not tucked in. The close-lying coat tends to be longer in kittens; it should not be springy.

The sepia colour of the coat is produced by dark brown ticking on a warm old ivory ground colour, with light bands next to the skin and dark tips. The muzzle, chin, chest and stomach are the colour of unbleached muslin. There is barring on the inner front legs and back knee only, but a dark line along the spine is not a fault, and the tail has a dark tip which extends back towards the body on the upper side. Nose leather is pale to dark salmon but must be outlined with dark brown, with dark brown eye rims and lips.

CARE TIP

Always make sure a cat has sufficient drinking water available. It curls its tongue into a spoon-like shape to lap, the rough surface helping to retain more liquid.

Longhaired Breeds

Turkish Angora

BODY

Medium size, long, graceful but firm and well-muscled, set on long slim legs, longer at the rear, with small oval paws; tail long and tapering.

HEAD

Long, wide between the ears, narrowing to a fine muzzle with no whisker break; in profile wedge-shaped, without a stop, neither round nor pointed and avoiding exaggerated type; ears large, pricked, wide at base, set high and continuing the lines of the wedge.

EYES

Large, almond-shaped and slanting, with good width between, green in all except for blue-eyed and odd-eyed whites to comply with GCCF standard but the CFA standard requires amber instead of green.

COAT

Medium long, longer on ruff, very fine with a silk-like sheen, full brush and tufts on ears.

COLOUR

The GCCF recognizes the same range of colours and patterns as for the Oriental Shorthairs, the CFA any colour and pattern except for chocolate, lavender and those with pointed coats.

Although the Angora cat was known in western Europe from the sixteenth century or earlier (they were seen at shows in the early days of the Cat Fancy); in later years they were overtaken in breeders' preference by the Persian, and in the twentieth century the breed disappeared from everywhere except its native land. It was revived after World War Two with cats exported from Ankara (old name Angora) in Turkey, where the Zoo had set up a breeding programme, to North America, Britain and Scandinavia. It was granted full Championship status in the USA in the early 1970s under the name Turkish Angora. The Angora recognized by the GCCF in Britain is a different breed.

The Turkish Angora's long, svelte body, and slender tail, its wedge-shaped head and oriental eyes present a quite different appearance from the longer-furred Persian cat. The coat is very fine and silky, with none of the woolly undercoat found in the Persian, and only medium long, although long fur would not be considered a fault. It has a wavy tendency but should lie flat along the body except around the chin, neck, underside and tail; it is longer at the ruff and should be plume-like on the tail. The tail is carried lower than the body but not trailing, though when moving the relaxed tail is brought forward horizontally over the body, sometimes almost touching the head.

When first re-established many people thought of the Angora only as a white cat and some bodies accepted no other colour. Now, a wide range of colours and patterns are recognized.

Turkish Van

BODY

Long and sturdy, males particularly muscular and strong, medium long legs with neat well-rounded feet, the tail of a length to balance the body.

HEAD

A short wedge shape with a long straight nose that has a barely perceptible dip in profile, large ears set high and fairly close together.

EYES

Large and oval; light amber, blue or odd-eyed; pink rims.

COAT

Long, soft and silky to the roots, no woolly undercoat, full brush to the tail, ears well feathered and tufts on the paws.

COLOURS

White patterned with auburn or with cream.

The cats which the people of the Lake Van area of Anatolia in Turkey consider their local cat are elegant all-white Angoras, with odd-eyed cats particularly prized, but the breed known in the western Cat Fancy as the Van is a patterned cat and was developed from cats with attractive auburn markings which an English breeder discovered when travelling in Turkey and took back to Britain in the 1950s.

The type is very much that of the Angora, although the standard specifies a slight dip in the profile of the head.

The coat must be chalk white with no trace of yellow. Auburn or cream markings should appear on the face, but not below the level of the eyes or beyond the base of the rear of the ears; they should be separated by a vertical white blaze leaving a white nose. The ears should be white with delicate shell pink inside. The tail also carries colour, faintly ringed, with the colour allowed to extend a short way up the back. Small auburn or cream 'thumb-prints' are permitted on the body fur but are not desirable and must be irregularly placed. The Van cat's coat will be longer and heavier in winter.

BREED CHARACTERISTIC

The Turkish Van has become known as the 'swimming cat' because it seems happy to dabble in streams or swim in pools or in the waters of Lake Van. Despite its length its fur dries unmatted.

Persian

This Blue Colourpoint Persian shows the Siamese pointed pattern transferred to a cat with long fur and the full Persian conformation.

A Red Self Persian. Though tabby markings are difficult to breed out in all red cats, they are far less noticeable when broken up by long fur.

The Persian longhaired cat is said to have arrived in western Europe from what is now Iran in the sixteenth century. In fact, although there are cats from further north with long fur, such as the Norwegian and Russian cats, it is not certain that these Persian cats were originally very different from the Angora and they may already have owed their differences to human selection rather than accidental development. It would be difficult, if not impossible, for cats with their fine, very long fur to survive except as pets helped in their grooming.

Their popularity in the early days of the Cat Fancy quite eclipsed the Angora, and the Persian itself began to be selected for ever longer fur and the flatter face which breeders found attractive. The trend continued, reaching its extreme in the Peke-faced Persian, a breed recognized only in North America, created to emulate the flat-faced look of the Pekingese dog. The changed bone structure and extreme foreshortening of the muzzle can bring problems in respiration, dentition and in the working of the tear ducts. The normal Persian breed should never be so flat nosed.

The modern Persian, or Longhair, as many of its colour varieties are known in Britain under the GCCF, is a medium to large cat of very stocky build, having a rather massive head with the characteristic short snub nose and big round eyes. It has a thick undercoat and a long topcoat which is very fine and of equal length all over the body except for the immense ruff which frames the face. The long hair on the tail forms a full brush and there are tufts on the ears and between the toes.

BODY

Large or medium size, of cobby type, well-muscled with a broad deep chest, massive across shoulders and rump, set on short thick legs with large round paws; the tail is short and bushy.

HEAD

Round and massive with broad skull, small round-tipped ears set low and wide apart, round forehead, full cheeks and a short broad nose of even width and with a definite stop, all on a short thick neck.

EYES

Large, round and set wide apart. Colour copper or deep orange for most coat colours – except for Whites which may be blue, orange or odd-eyed, Chinchillas, Shaded Silvers and Golden Persians which should be emerald green or blue-green, Silver Tabbies green or hazel, Chocolate Tabbies hazel or copper and Colourpoints blue.

◄ *A Seal Colourpoint Persian.*
Colourpoints, originally known
in the USA as Himalayans,
differ from the other Persians
in having blue eyes.

Persian cats are recognized in the whole range of cat colours and patterns. The CFA groups them all as one breed, while the GCCF divides them into several separate classes according to the type of coat pattern, with the pointed cats known as Colourpoints, a group which some American bodies class separately as Himalayans (see page 80), while solid colour lilac and chocolate have been classed separately by some American bodies as Kashmirs. American taste is for a more extreme type than is considered acceptable in Britain.

Most Persian cats are gentle, placid pets that make few demands upon their owners but they do need regular and thorough grooming to keep their coats in condition and free of tangles.

CARE TIP

Persian cats need grooming at least once every day.
Use a metal comb with widely spaced teeth to get
the legs free of tangles then go on to the belly, flanks,
back, chest, neck and tail. Always move the comb
upwards so that the hair stands out. For the shorter
facial hair use a fine-toothed comb or a toothbrush.
Next brush the coat, again working upwards. Groom
your cat on a sheet of newspaper to catch any dirt or
flea debris which may be combed out.

COAT

Long, thick, fine and soft
but not excessively woolly,
standing out from the body
and with a full frill covering
the shoulders and continuing
in a deep frill between the
front legs.

COLOURS

All recognized cat colours and
patterns including selfs,
different levels of tipping,
tri- bi- and Van bi-colours and
pointed patterns in white,
black, blue, red, cream,
chocolate, silver, gold, brown,
seal, and lilac. See Himalayan
(page 80).

LONGHAIRED BREEDS

*T*he sparkling Chinchilla Persian, sometimes known in the USA as the Silver Persian, displays a silky top coat tipped with black and eyes oulined in black, which make it one of the most beautiful of cats. Early Chinchillas had darker tipping than modern cats. ▶

A Tortoiseshell Persian. Its three colours of black, red and cream pattern the fur on the body, legs and head. A cream or red blaze on the face is often considered desirable. ▶

LONGHAIRED BREEDS

Himalayan

*I*t was under the name Himalayan that the American equivalent of the Colourpoint Persians of Europe was first recognized by the United States registries in the late 1950s and early 1960s. The CFA now places it as a colour variety of the Persian. However, although standards on both sides of the Atlantic are similar, American taste is for a much more extreme interpretation than would be acceptable in Britain and Europe.

The application of a pointed pattern to a Persian type cat took place separately in the USA and Europe. The first conscious breeding for cats of this type was probably in Sweden in the 1920s, followed by work in Massachusetts in the next decade, but it was not until the 1950s that the breed was developed in California under the name Himalayan. Meanwhile, British breeders had begun their experiments in the 1930s. British stock provided the basis for Canadian and European lines.

The Himalayan and Colourpoint Persians follow the basic standards for the Persian, but with the pointed pattern and blue eyes of Siamese cats.

CAT BEHAVIOUR

A cat with its ears flattened sideways is being submissive, but if the body is tense and pressed to the ground it is frightened. The ears moving backward, showing more of their rear side, indicate its latent aggression and a readiness to defend itself.

BODY

Large or medium size, of cobby type, well-muscled with a broad deep chest, massive across shoulders and rump, set on short thick legs with large round paws; tail short and bushy.

HEAD

Round and massive with broad skull, small round-tipped ears set low and wide apart, round forehead, full cheeks and a short broad nose of even width and with a definite stop, all on a short thick neck.

EYES

Large, round and set wide apart. Blue only.

COAT

Long, thick, fine and soft but not excessively woolly, standing out from the body and with a full frill covering the shoulders and continuing in a deep frill between the front legs.

COLOURS

Siamese pattern and colours.

Longhair Scottish Fold

The Longhair Scottish Fold is at present recognized by one cat registration body only: The International Cat Association (TICA). ▶

BODY

Medium size, rounded with no thickening of legs or tail. Long tapering tail preferred. Neat paws with well-rounded toes.

HEAD

Well-rounded with firm chin and jaw; well-rounded whisker pads. Short nose. Small ears with rounded tips, folded forward and down.

EYES

Large, well-rounded and separated by a broad nose, wide open and with a sweet expression.

COAT

Soft, dense and plush, so thick it stands away from the body.

COLOUR

Any cat coat and pattern except for chocolate and lavender (lilac) and those with darker Siamese-type points.

The longhaired Scottish Fold was recognized by the International Cat Association (TICA) but this is the only registration body to accept the breed, although the Longhaired Scottish Fold has been bred in Britain and the USA.

The breed had its origin in a drop-eared kitten, one of a litter of cats with normal ears, born on a farm in Scotland, from which the shorthaired Scottish fold was developed. This breed comes from the same stock as the shorthaired type and it has a similar conformation but, of course, with long fur. A medium-sized cat, it has a sturdy, well-rounded body, even along its length carrying a round head with prominent cheeks on a short neck. The ears are set in a cap-like fashion to expose a rounded cranium. They are comparatively small and fold forward and downward. A tightly folded ear is preferred to a loose fold and a large ear. At birth the ears are pricked, the drop not becoming apparent until the kittens are about a month old.

A wide range of colours is accepted. Eye colour should be as appropriate to the dominant colour of the fur.

CARE TIP

The claws of an indoor cat may grow too long. Trim them with strong nail clippers. Squeeze the paw pad slightly to make the claws protrude and snip across the claw tip, keeping well clear of the quick, the pink area which is suffused with blood.

Maine Coon

◄ *The Maine Coon, originating as a rugged farm cat able to withstand Maine winters, makes an amiable pet.*

A Brown Tabby and White Maine Coon cat used to be the variety most frequently seen but many other coat colours and patterns are now bred. ►

BODY

Medium to large, long, muscular and broad chested with a square rump, presenting a rectangular appearance; substantial medium long legs with large round paws; tail at least as long as back and tapering.

HEAD

Medium long and slightly less wide, the nasal bridge equidistant from the ear line and the nose tip; muzzle square, chin firm, cheekbones high and cheeks fairly full, nose slightly concave in profile and without a sharp break or stop; ears large, pointed, wide-based and set high but well apart; the neck moderately long and particularly thick in males.

EYES

Large, round and wide-set, slightly oblique in aperture and set. Shades of green, gold or copper; blue or odd-eyed with white fur.

COAT

Heavy and shaggy, silky in texture and falling smoothly.

COLOURS

Self, tipped, tabby and particolour in white, black, blue, red, cream, silver.

The Maine Coon cat is the earliest of the breeds developed in the United States. The name comes from the mistaken belief of some settlers that it resulted from a cross between a domestic cat and a raccoon – a mating impossible in nature. It has some similarity with the Norwegian Forest Cat and perhaps can trace its origins back to a cat taken to the USA by the early Viking settlers but it may possibly have descended from crosses between the early domestic arrivals and later introductions of Angoras, toughened up by harsh winters on the farms of the eastern seaboard. It was a popular breed in the early days of the American Cat Fancy but disappeared from shows with the growing fashion for Persian cats until the Central Maine Coon Cat Club was founded in 1953 to revive the breed. It was again given recognition with full championship status in 1967.

The Maine Coon's rugged, muscular appearance is a reminder of its evolution as a working farm cat. Its heavy, shaggy, weatherproof coat, the undercoat covered by a more substantial glossy topcoat, which helps it withstand the Maine winter, is virtually self-maintaining. Nowhere as long as in the Persian, the fur is shorter on the head, neck and shoulders, increasingly long on the back, flanks and tail, with breeches and belly fur full and shaggy and a noticeable frontal ruff beginning at the base of the ears.

This breed has an amiable disposition and is recognized in a wide range of colours and patterns. Eye colour does not have to match the coat.

Norwegian Forest Cat

BODY

Large, sturdy, with a longish body carried high on the legs, the hind legs higher than the front ones; long tail reaching back at least to the shoulder blades.

HEAD

Triangular with a long straight profile, without a break in line, the muzzle gently rounded and a strong chin; ears high and open, wide at the base and high set so that the space between them is less than the width of one ear.

EYES

Large, slightly oblique, all colours regardless of coat colour.

COAT

Semi-long, a woolly undercoat covered by a glossy water-repellent overcoat on back and sides. Long full ruff, shirtfront, knickerbockers, bushy tail and lynx-like ear tufts with inner feathering.

COLOURS

All colours and patterns except chocolate, lilac and Siamese point pattern.

*T*he Norwegian Forest Cat, Norsk Skaukatt (or Skogkatt) to give its native name, is another hardy breed that developed as a farm cat. It was not until the 1930s that Norwegian breeders gave it attention and it was 1972 before it got its first Norwegian standards and 1977 before it became a FIFe championship breed.

A large and solidly-built cat, its semi-long topcoat is water-repellent. Its physical similarities suggest links with the Maine Coon and the Siberian. Affectionate pets, they usually inherit the confidence and resourcefulness of their ancestors. A wide range of coat colours and patterns are recognized. Kittens are born with short, soft fur. The tough guard hair topcoat develops as the cat matures and is shorter in summer. Norwegian Forest Cats may not reach full muscular development until they are four to five years old.

Similar cats are found in Denmark and Sweden where they go under the names Racekatte and Rugkatt.

CAT BEHAVIOUR

Cats have a strong sense of balance and can quickly right themselves when falling to land on all fours. However, though their feet can usually cushion the fall, the impetus on landing may bring the jaw hard onto the ground and fracture the palate. Discourage cats from sleeping on windowsills and parapets.

Siberian Forest Cat

The Siberian Cat, a Russian breed only recently seen elsewhere, may be the ancestor of both the similar Scandanavian breeds and the Middle Eastern longhairs. ▶

BODY

Strong and sturdy; longish body set on strong legs, tail reaches back almost to the shoulders.

HEAD

A broad skull, the equilateral triangle of the face softened by rounded contours but with a straight profile; high set, wide-based ears.

EYES

Large, not quite round and slightly oblique; colour in keeping with coat, being hazel to green with the golden tabby coat which is most usually seen.

COAT

Long with a glossy top coat and thick insulating undercoat, full ruff, breeches and tail.

COLOURS

Many varieties are under development, but a golden tabby with black patterning over a golden agouti is currently the best known.

*I*t seems likely that the mutation for long hair may have occurred originally in eastern Russia or Siberia and spread from there to Persia and Turkey, as well as westwards to create the longhaired Scandinavian cats. The longhair gene is present in as many as 64 per cent of cats in St Petersburg and occurs right across to the Pacific where it is found in 21 per cent of cats; these territories have been much less affected by deliberate breeding policies than in countries where the Cat Fancy became well established. Kittens are born with short fur, the glossy guard hairs appearing by the time they are three months old.

In the early days of cat shows Russian longhairs appeared on the show bench and one was owned by Harrison Weir but it is only recently that interest has been revived with the development of a Cat Fancy in Russia and the exhibition of the breed at the International Cat Show in New York in 1991.

The Siberian differs from the Maine Coon and from the Norwegian Forest Cat in having a rounder head.

CAT BEHAVIOUR

Faced with a threat, a cat will make its fur stand on end and arch its back, making itself look a more formidable opponent.

Birman

◀ *A Sealpoint Birman, the original colour form of the Sacred Cat of Burma. A legend claims it was a temple cat, whose blue eyes, golden coat and white paws were given by a goddess.*

Tradition says these were ancient Burmese temple cats, who miraculously acquired their white paws and golden dusted coat. There are various claims as to when they were first taken to Europe but they were certainly in France by 1920, recognized there under the name Sacred Cat of Burma in 1925 and developed by French breeders, not reaching the USA until 1959 – nor Britain until 1964.

Though this strong and muscular cat combines point markings with long fur it should look neither like a Siamese nor a Persian but has its own distinctive appearance. The Birman pattern consists of dark points as in the Siamese but the paws have white 'gloves', which on the front paws end in an even line across the paw at or before the angle formed by the paw and leg; on the back feet they cover all the paw and taper up the back of the leg, not going beyond the hock.

The coat of the original seal colour is a clear beige with a golden hue and the CFA standard asks for a 'golden mist' on the back and sides of blue, chocolate and lilac coats as well (the extent of its colour range). The GCCF expects any body tints to be as in similar colour Siamese, though a warm-toned shading across the shoulders is also favoured by breeders.

CAT PHYSIOLOGY

Cats can run very fast for short distances only. Their digestive organs take up a lot of space and they do not have big hearts and lungs.

BODY

Long and massive, set on heavy, medium-long legs with big strong round paws; tail medium long.

HEAD

Broad rounded skull, medium long nose with a slight dip but no stop, slightly convex; full cheeks, rounded muzzle and a strong chin; ears medium high, almost as wide as tall, spaced well apart and as much to the side as the top of the head.

EYES

Almost round, the outer corner tilted very slightly upward, set well apart; blue, the deeper the better.

COAT

Medium to long, silky and non-matting with a heavy ruff, slight curls on the stomach, short on the face but longer on the outer edge of the cheeks.

COLOURS

Seal, blue, chocolate, lilac, red and cream solid points and tortie, tabby and tortie-tabby variations on these, but only seal, blue, chocolate and lilac in CFA.

Ragdoll

The Ragdoll, shunned when it was thought at risk from lack of sensitivity to pain and danger, is now gaining in popularity. ▶

BODY

Long body with strong bone, not cobby like the Persian, set on strong legs with large paws and with a long tail.

HEAD

Broad between the ears as in the Birman and Persian; in profile the forehead sloping to a rounded chin with a slight dip between the eyes; wide-based, medium-sized slightly rounded ears.

EYES

Almost round and slightly oblique, bright china blue.

COAT

A thick silky topcoat of medium length over a shorter silky undercoat; with ruff, breeches and a plumed tail.

COLOURS

Seal, blue, chocolate and lilac pointed patterns, plus red, cream and torties of all these in Britain; always with a point pattern, either with white paws as in the Birman (plus a white band from chin to undertail and a white chin), colourpoint or bi-colour with the points and other white markings.

Originating in a mating between a Birman male and a white longhaired female, the Ragdoll gets its name from the tendency of the breed to relax when handled, like a child's ragdoll, a condition the original breeder attributed to injuries sustained by the mother in a traffic accident, despite the fact that such incidents do not result in genetic mutation. It was also claimed that the breed lacked the instinct of fear and did not feel pain like other cats, factors which made it unacceptable to many cat lovers until shown to be erroneous. It was first recognized in the USA by the National Cat Fanciers Association (NCFA) in 1965 and in Britain by the Cat Association of Britain in 1983.

The Ragdoll is a large animal which is as strong and healthy as other cats. It differs from other breeds in that the standards allow a loose fatty area on the belly.

Originally only cats with a coat pattern like that of the Birman were accepted but now these 'mitted' cats have been joined by the Colourpoint/Himalayans and the Bi-colours. On Bi-colours an inverted white 'V' on the face is considered important, and some societies also allow it in the mitted pattern.

CARE TIP

There are plenty of special cat toys on the market but a piece of string, a table tennis ball or a crumpled piece of paper can provide lots of fun without emptying your purse.

Somali

◄ *A Blue Somali kitten, at four months old. The Somali is a medium-longhaired version of the Abyssinian cat.*

An adult Sorrel (or Red) Somali, with chocolate-ticked copper fur over apricot base fur. ►

BODY

Foreign type but more solid looking than the Siamese, well developed and muscular with slim legs and oval feet; tail fairly long, thick at base and tapering.

HEAD

A moderate, slightly rounded wedge; brow, cheeks and profile showing a gentle contour and flowing into the arched neck without a break; the muzzle not sharply pointed, a shallow indentation forming the muzzle desirable but a pinch a fault; a slight nose break and a firm chin; ears set well apart, pricked, broad and cupped at base.

EYES

Large, bright and almond-shaped, neither round nor fully oriental; green or gold in colour, plus hazel in the GCCF standard and amber to yellow in some others.

COAT

A double coat, very soft to the touch; medium long, except on head, very fine and dense, at least three bands of ticking and often many more.

COLOURS

Ruddy, blue, sorrel, lilac, fawn; also chocolate and all these in tortie and with silver in some cat associations.

The name of this longhaired version of the Abyssinian indicates its association, for Somalia shares a border with Ethiopia (Abyssinia). Though longhaired kittens had previously occured in Abyssinian litters, and one was exhibited in Australia in 1965, it was only in 1967 that an American breeder first decided to develop a new breed. They reached Europe ten years later.

In conformation the Somali follows the Abyssinian precisely, being neither cobby nor oriental in type, the head less rounded than the British or American Shorthairs but not nearly so pointed as the Siamese and other orientals. The coat has the same darker shading on the spine, tail and heels, facial marks and dark eye line. The long hairs are ticked through their length – some have as many as fourteen bands, with the tip dark; light tips are a fault. Head hair is short, that on the body of medium length with a good ruff, breeches are preferred, and a full tail; ears are tufted and there are tufts between the toes.

Kittens often have rather dark coats, the agouti ticking becoming more apparent with maturity.

A variation on the Somali, exhibited at a CA of Britain show in 1990, is the Suqutranese, which has the conformation and coat characteristics of the Somali but with dazzling white, unticked fur.

Balinese

*T*his is the longhaired version of the Siamese cat, named the Balinese because Siamese breeders disliked the use of the name Siamese Longhair and because a southeast Asian name, which also recalled the dancers of the Indonesian island, seemed appropriate. Breeding began in the USA in the late 1940s but it was not until 20 years later that recognition was given by most American associations and more than another decade before it was recognized in Europe.

The Balinese follows the Siamese conformation and is identical in all details except coat length, but the longer fur gives the appearance of softer lines and less extreme type. Unusually among the semi-longhair breeds the GCCF standard specifically expresses a preference for no neck frill or ruff.

The breed inherits the inquisitive, talkative nature of the Siamese and its rather harsh call, and is usually very playful with its offspring.

Kittens are born with short coats and without point markings, and, as with Siamese the colour appears in the first weeks of life but the full coat may not develop until they are fully adult.

The CFA excludes tabby, tortie, red and cream varieties from the breed and groups them separately under the name Javanese, a name used by other registries for quite different cats.

BODY

Medium size, lithe and graceful, set on long slim legs, hind legs longer than the front, with small oval feet; a long, thin tapering tail.

HEAD

A long tapering wedge narrowing to a fine muzzle, flaring out to the tips of the ears to form a triangle with no break at the whiskers, with a strong chin and set on an elegant neck; large pricked ears, wide at the base, width between the eyes.

EYES

Almond-shaped and slanting towards the nose; clear blue in colour.

COAT

Fine, silky and medium long without any woolly undercoat.

COLOURS

Seal, blue, chocolate and lilac are the only colours to be recognized by the CFA; other associations add red, cream and tortie, tabby and tortie-tabby variations of these colours and some an even greater range.

Javanese

BODY

Medium size, lithe and graceful, set on long slim legs, hind legs longer than the front, with small oval feet; a long, thin tapering tail.

HEAD

A long tapering wedge narrowing to a fine muzzle, flaring out to the tips of the ears to form a triangle with no break at the whiskers, with a strong chin and set on an elegant neck; large pricked ears, wide at the base, width between the eyes.

EYES

Almond-shaped and slanting towards the nose; bright green for solid and all-over patterns, clear blue for CFA pointed cats.

COAT

Fine, silky and medium long without any woolly undercoat.

COLOURS

Black, blue, chocolate, cinnamon, lilac, fawn, red, cream, tortie, tabby, tipped and silver varieties, though restricted in some associations. CFA red, cream and tortie and lynx (tabby) patterns of these and their Balinese colours.

Javanese is the name given to longhaired cats of oriental type by associations which are members of the FIFe and by some other bodies. The name reflects its closeness to the Balinese of which it is an unpointed equivalent (except for in the CFA). In Britain, where the difficulties of quarantine and other problems made it difficult to import Turkish Angora cats, a similar longhair resulting from an Abyssinian/Siamese breeding programme was the starting point for the creation of an equivalent of the Turkish Angora. However, at a later stage the breeding programme moved towards a more oriental type and is now recognized by the CA of Britain as being a white Javanese. The GCCF retains the name Angora but it remains a more oriental cat than the Turkish Angora and is not descended from the original Turkish line.

Javanese and the GCCF's Angora are slender oriental cats and recognized in a wide range of colours and patterns, although not all are recognized by all associations.

Alternative names are Oriental Longhair and Mandarin, while many British breeders still call them 'Cuckoo' cats, after the nickname given to the cat from which the British strain have stemmed.

In the CFA, the Javanese is the name used to describe cats of red, tortie or tabby varieties which other associations recognize as Balinese.

Asian Longhair/Tiffany

◄ *A Silver-tipped Tiffany, a semi-longhaired version of the Burmese. Some associations restrict the use of the name to Asian Longhairs which show the full Burmese colour restriction.*

The Tiffany is the longhaired version of the Burmese cat, some of which appeared in the United States in 1970, but similar semi-longhaired cats have also been produced in Britain as part of the Asian Group breeding programme which produced the Burmilla. In some associations Tiffany applies strictly to those with a Burmese shaded coat but the GCCF, which spells the name Tiffanie, uses it for solid or Burmese restricted coats in a wide range of colours. The CA of Britain recognizes the whole range as Asian Longhairs, with Tiffany used as the name for restricted coat cats within the breed.

All the Asian Longhairs have a Burmese conformation, showing the usual differences of a somewhat heavier type in the USA and a lighter boned type in Britain and the rest of Europe.

These are reputed to be rather bossy cats, with quite strident voices when they want to get attention.

CARE TIP

Help cats to remove worn covering from their claws, to stretch and exercise – and prevent damage to your furnishings – by providing a scratching post or a panel of coarse carpet (of a rough texture and not like your furnishings). Train them to use it by carrying them there whenever they begin to scratch. Hold their paws and move them in a scratching motion on the post.

BODY

Compact, medium length and size with an ample rounded chest, back level from shoulder to tail, slender legs, with round toes in the USA, oval in Britain, tail straight and medium long; heavier than it looks.

HEAD

Rounded on top with wide cheekbones and tapering to a short blunt wedge with a firm chin, all planes are rounded and there is a distinct nose break, eyes well apart, ears broad based with rounded tips and tilting slightly forward; all set on a well-developed neck.

EYES

Large and rounded, but GCCF Tiffanies with the upper line a straight oriental slant; colour green for all Asian Longhairs other than Tiffany, which are golden; for most Tiffanies any shade of yellow with golden preferred, with green preferred for silvers.

COAT

Long, fine, and silky, longer and fuller on tail, breeches and ruff.

COLOURS

Brown (sable), blue, chocolate, lilac, red, cream, tortie, tabby and tipped versions of these and all colours of silver.

Cymric

The Cymric is the longhaired version of the Manx cat. As in the Manx, a double inheritance of two dominant genes for taillessness is fatal.

▶

BODY

Solid and compact with a broad chest and short back ending in a round rump, higher than the shoulder; short, sturdy front legs and much longer back legs, paws neat and round. In fully tailless Cymric there should be no bone or cartilage interfering with the roundness of the rump.

HEAD

Round, with prominent cheeks, broad nose and a strong muzzle; wide ears with open base and rounded tip are angled slightly outwards.

EYES

Large and round, the CFA specifying they be set at a slight angle to the nose. Any colour in accordance with coat colour plus green, gold, copper, blue and odd-eyed.

COAT

Thick and harsh, long top-coat over an even thicker, woolly undercoat.

COLOUR

All colours, combinations and patterns except that some registration bodies do not accept Siamese type points patterns.

The Cymric is a longhaired version of the Manx. Its name is the word in the Welsh language for Wales and was chosen to suggest proximity to the Isle of Man, for which the Manx is named. Though both short and longhaired forms of the Manx are known on the Isle of Man it was not until longhaired kittens appeared in Canadian litters in the 1960s that the Cymric was developed as a breed.

Although the Cymric has a conformation identical to that of the Manx in every respect except for its coat, it often looks a larger animal because the heavier padding of its undercoat, especially when it lives in colder areas, gives the impression of greater bulk. Cymrics have a reputation for quiet voices and confident personalities.

As in the Manx, Cymric kittens may occur without tails (rumpy), with vestigal cartilage only tails (rumpy-riser), stump tails (stumpy), short but otherwise normal tails (longy), and full tails. Similarly, the combination of two Manx genes is fatal and kittens die at the foetal stage.

CAT BEHAVIOUR

Most domestic cats can jump five times their own height with ease. They will often aim a little way below the top of a wall and 'run' up the last section. Jumping down, a cat will often reach down the vertical surface before pushing out into the air, reducing the length of the fall and thereby lessening the impact with the ground.

New Breeds

More than 45 breeds of cat are described in this book and within most breeds there is a range of colour varieties although breeders continue to seek new permutations of colour and form. The range of cat breeds is certainly not exhausted and some of those in development may well have gained official acceptance by the time you read this book.

There is the Seychellois for instance, which has been bred in both longhair and shorthair forms. The Seychellois Shorthair was the result of a breeding programme, registered with the CA of Britain in 1988, which was designed to transfer to British cats a pattern of white coat with patches of colour and a solid colour tail that appeared as an endemic form on the Seychelles islands. Although the pattern is similar to that of the Turkish Van, it is less restricted. The Seychellois is an attractive, medium-sized cat of oriental conformation with long slim legs and oval paws, wedge-shaped head with wide-set, pointed ears and almond-shaped eyes of brilliant blue. Its short and silky coat is bred with the colour distributed in three different ways: the Septième, with large splashes of colour on the flanks, legs and head, the Huitième, having smaller splashes of colour with a similar distribution, and the Neuvième, with splashes on the head and legs but not on the body.

The Seychellois originated with two tortie and white Persian cats and cats of oriental type, and they inherit the Siamese personality traits of the oriental side of their ancestry. Both the longhaired and the shorthaired Sechellois developed with the same three types of colour distribution and the same general oriental conformation, the difference being that in the Sechellois Longhair the fur is long, fine and silky, lying close on the body but with a slightly longer ruff, the ears are well feathered and the tail is plumed. The coats of both the Seychellois Longhair and the Seychellois Shorthair may combine white with markings of any other colour except black. As in the Siamese, their kittens are born white and their colour patterning develops slowly. In genetically red varieties it may not be fully developed until they are three years old.

On the other side of the world the Spotted Mist is the first breed to have been created entirely in Australia. This breed, which gained full recognition in 1987 – though only in the state of New South Wales – was developed from crosses between Burmese and Abyssinian cats with the addition of some domestic tabby, in a breeding programme that began in the late 1970s. It is a medium-sized cat of only moderately foreign type, with large lustrous green eyes that range from green to ultramarine. Its short, close-lying, easy-to-care-for coat has an overall ticking, creating a misty background of a creamy mushroom shade. This is patterned with delicate but distinct spots of either brown, blue, chocolate, lilac or caramel (with further colours from the Burmese range being developed). Legs and tail are ringed and the face carries the usual tabby markings. These are claimed to be outstandingly affectionate and gentle cats which also retain excellent mousing skills.

Another recently developed breed, at the time of writing recognized only by The International Cat Association (TICA), which tends to be more accepting of new breeds than other associations, is the Californian Spangled. This is a spotted cat developed from a mixture of Siamese, Angora, silver tabby, spotted Manx, a domestic/Abyssinian cross and a shorthaired cat from Malaysia. It was created partly to provide a spotted cat which would appeal to people who had been attracted to the idea of trying to keep spotted wild species, and to provide an alternative to discourage them from doing so. Its difference from the other spotted breeds perhaps lies less in its appearance than in the fact that it was launched in the Christmas catalogue of the Neiman Marcus store in California at a price of $1400!

TICA also recognize a longhaired form of the Russian Blue under the neame of Nebelung. A Longhair Scottish Fold (see page 81) is on its way to becoming an established breed and a white-coated version of the Somali, the Suqutranese, has also appeared in Britain.

The Celonese, originally developed in the Cat Club of Ceylon and is now being bred in Italy. It is a ticked tabby with barred legs and looks rather similar to the Abyssinians shown at the end of the last century. Another cat with barring on legs and tail, and provisionally known as the Wild Abyssinian, has been developed from a feral cat from Singapore.

A new breed, which has been taken up in Denmark, is the Sokoke Cat, a cat with tabby markings of a particular kind, found in the Sokoke area of Kenya. This may be a mutation of a local domestic cat but is just possibly a local subspecies of *Felis silvestris* or a hybrid of the wild cat with feral domestic cats.

More controversial is a cat which has been dubbed the Munchkin, after the little people in The Wizard of Oz. It was exhibited in 1991 at TICA's Madison Square Garden Show. It is a mutant form in which leg length is reduced – the effect of a gene like the one which produces the Dachshund. Will the cat world generally tolerate such a change in the cat's appearance? If it does, you could eventually see every one of the breeds in this book duplicated in a short-legged form.

PHOTOGRAPHIC ACKNOWLEDGEMENTS

All photographs by Ray Moller, except those listed below.

The publishers would like to thank the agencies and photographers who supplied us with the photographs reproduced on the following pages:

The Ancient Art & Architecture Collection 12, 13; Animal House Fotos/Excalibur, Milan (Bob Schwartz) 37, 40, 48, 74; Ardea, London/J.P. Ferrero 47; Bruce Coleman Ltd 10 (Hans Reinhard), 52 (Jane Burton); The Cat Fanciers' Association, Inc., N.J., U.S.A. 19; Cogis, Versailles 30 (Lanceau), 39 (Lanceau), 53 (Excalibur), 80 (Français); Marc Henrie 22, 23, 31, 85; Mansell Collection Ltd 18; Mary Evans Picture Library 16; NHPA 11 (Nigel Dennis), 38 (Gerard Lacz), 68 (Gerard Lacz), 81 (Gerard Lacz); Solitaire Photographic/Angela Rixon 36; Werner Forman Archive Ltd/ British Museum 17

The publishers would also like to thank Sue Boorman who arranged for the cats to be photographed, and to all the cat owners who so kindly cooperated.